Jennie M... psycho-therapist, t... ...0 years' experience ... ...-to-one with personality disorders, and seeing couples. She is also the founder of the very popular 'The Key to Couples Work', a TA-based training programme ... ... delivers in this coun... ...broa... ...work... ... ...e Armed Forces training their welfare officers, a... ...s currently designing a training programme for solicitors' practices and other professional offices. In her private practice, she sees individuals for long-term psychotherapy, couples and small family groups. Jennie is well known internationally for her work in relationships and creative use of boundaries.

Victoria Lambert is an international award-winning journalist, and has written for most of the UK's national newspapers, principally the *Daily Telegraph*, the *Guardian* and the *Daily Mail*. She has written for numerous magazines including *Woman & Home*, *The Spectator* and *Saga*, and has been a columnist for *Geographical* and education magazine *School House* where she is the agony aunt. Staff positions have included Health Editor of the *Daily Telegraph* and Health Editor of the *Daily Mail*, plus Foreign Editor, in Australia, of the *Sydney Daily Telegraph*. Victoria Lambert's work is syndicated worldwide and she has been recognised with awards including the Best Cancer Reporter Award 2011 presented by the European School of Oncology.

Boundaries

How to Draw the Line in Your Head, Heart and Home

Jennie Miller and Victoria Lambert

ONE PLACE. MANY STORIES

HQ
An imprint of HarperCollins*Publishers* Ltd
1 London Bridge Street
London SE1 9GF

This paperback edition 2019

1
First published in Great Britain by
HQ, an imprint of HarperCollins*Publishers* Ltd 2019

A catalogue record for this book is
available from the British Library.

ISBN: 978-0-00-827160-2

Printed and bound in Great Britain by
CPI Group (UK) Ltd, Croydon, CR0 4YY

MIX
Paper from
responsible sources
FSC™ C007454

This book is produced from independently certified FSC™ paper
to ensure responsible forest management.

For more information visit: www.harpercollins.co.uk/green

Contents

Introduction

Do you often feel you can't say no? Do you feel spread too thinly between work, emotional relationships and family, and your responsibilities and chores? Perhaps you feel overloaded with to-do lists, promises to friends, financial obligations, or that intangible pressure to succeed in everything you do all at the same time. You may feel frustrated that there is never any time to do those things that really matter to you – whether it is to write a book, spend unpressured time with your loved ones, or just be alone guilt-free. With demands coming from all sides, it is surprisingly easy these days to get buffeted along without ever really feeling in control.

Yet, there is an alternative to living in this twenty-first-century chaos – a way of reframing your own attitude and behaviour so that you can take charge of your life and not allow others undue influence or control. A process which will enable you to improve your quality of life (at work, home and play); to build self-respect; and to lead to a healthier way of being on all levels.

The solution to all this is: boundaries. A complete concept that will allow you to reach past any obstacle and make real change happen in every area of your life.

What are boundaries? In short, these are the decisions we make which govern our own behaviour and the way we interact with others. A sort of personal code which may change with time and circumstance. We'll explain the concept of boundaries in more depth in the next section but for now hold in mind that a boundary is where you choose to draw a line in the sand in any scenario.

Why do they matter? Because we can't just follow patterns of behaviour that worked for previous generations as life on this planet has changed beyond recognition in the past thirty years. We are now a 24/7 culture, invisibly connected from our homes to the entire world.

We live in the fast lane, yet few of us have developed strategies to cope with the new problems that have arisen as a result. These issues include burgeoning social media, high-speed and high-turnover lovers, growing workloads in the face of new technology, constantly conflicting opinions on diet and health, and a culture of perfectionism in parenting and relationships. There are familiar problems too which many of us still struggle with: the impact of divorce, personality clashes, the stresses of being caught in the generation gap and career dilemmas.

But there is no doubt that the arrival of the Internet, consumer society, medical advances that are giving us decades of extra life and career expectations have changed life as older generations knew it beyond belief. The way we humans interact with each other has also undergone fundamental shifts, and we believe the way to regain our own equilibrium is to re-examine our lives and behaviour and use fresh boundaries in response to these new dilemmas.

With that in mind, we have devised a Four-Step Programme to teach the use of boundaries in everyday life, beginning with ourselves, and then exploring how the system works in situations related to every aspect of our lives: ourselves, our work life, our relationships and our family. We advise you to follow the Programme in the order set out in the book, although some may find particular sections are more resonant or urgent in their circumstances. Everyone, though, will benefit by starting with a closer look at themselves – and what we call our 'self-boundaries'.

What do we mean by that? Self-boundaries are the demarcations which define our behaviour, thoughts and feelings. They are that inner voice which says to us: 'Go this far but no further.' When used correctly, they help us modify our behaviour or relationships so that we feel or consider ourselves safe. And we need to get into the habit of caring for our 'selves' before we can build the healthy relationships with others that will see us thrive.

Each section of the book will contain exercises and sections called Bring in the Boundaries which contain practical tips on identifying and using boundaries, and offer anonymised case histories from Jennie's clinical practice to exemplify what you need to know. These examples help us to understand how boundaries work in specific circumstances, from dating to divorce, interacting with elderly parents to raising teenagers and managing a team to working for a fractious boss. (The situations chosen have been picked deliberately because in Jennie's experience they're the ones most people need help addressing and have the highest impact on lives.) Look out, too, for 'Draw the Line' moments – thoughts and phrases which will support and inspire you as you progress through the book.

There is no timescale for this book because we all work at our own pace, so don't feel you have to achieve this new state of being overnight. The first step towards a healthy you may well be in accepting that you can't change your life instantly. But as you read this you are already starting on that journey.

What are Boundaries?

Like many psychotherapists and proponents of healthy living, Jennie believes that learning to establish good boundaries is crucial to forming and keeping healthy relationships, with yourself and others. And you may well have heard the term 'boundaries' used out loud already – even if you don't really know what it means – phrases like 'I need to establish good boundaries for my child around bedtime' or someone telling you that 'your work–life balance needs some boundaries.'

But the need to understand and utilise boundaries has never been more acute, and existing advice doesn't cover many of the situations we now accept and deal with every day.

For example, our fast-paced lives require us to make more decisions than in the past, often quickly – yet with potentially serious consequences. The challenges to our boundaries are more complex and demanding, and we all need new strategies on how to live life as healthily as possible.

The effect of technology on our boundaries is particularly important when it comes to conversations and relationships. These used to be straightforward but now are more difficult because of the lack of face-to-face contact. Situations can easily be misread, moods can be misinterpreted and remarks can be misconstrued when you remove the physical presence of human contact.

The 24/7 culture of e-mails and the Internet means we can never switch off. We are no longer able to pull up the mental drawbridge – we are always vulnerable to what feels like outside pressures and invasions. Some of this attention is not unwelcome, we encourage it ourselves. But that doesn't mean our boundaries are healthy; it may mean we don't recognise what can hurt us.

The inspiration for this book came about through a conversation we shared on the subject of e-mail communication. In a steamy coffee shop full of post-school run parents and busy workers grabbing a latte to go, we found ourselves catching up on life, work, family and friends. During our chat, Victoria mentioned a familiar dilemma she was struggling with – she had been asked to help with a function which she had neither the time, energy, or the desire to do. However, she felt a strong pull to be useful and the resulting emotion was guilt. Jennie identified her problem as being a lack of boundaries and explained the concepts that underpin them (as we will explore in this book).

Victoria went home inspired and wrote an e-mail explaining to a colleague why she couldn't help at the function. She wrote:

'I am so sorry to say that I feel I cannot help with your plans towards putting on this event. I am really busy with work and childcare at the moment, so am finding it hard to make time. Obviously, I will still do what I can to be useful, and don't forget to ask me to invite those people we mentioned, but I think that will have to be my input for now. Do call if I can do anything else.'

Then she thought again about Jennie's explanation of boundaries, and realised she wasn't being honest. Moreover, she was soft-soaping her decision because she felt guilty – which was confusing the issue, not clarifying it. Several long phone calls with Jennie followed as Victoria was feeling uncomfortable and anxious about the potential response. Jennie encouraged her to be brave and brief.

This was her second draft (with self-boundary): *'I won't be available to help with your event. I know it will be a huge success, and wish you well.'*

And the response to that second e-mail: *'Fair enough. Thank you for letting me know. Do come if you can.'*

What Victoria found was that waiting for a response to a boundaried e-mail can feel nail-biting. However, as can be seen from the reply, others usually respond surprisingly well to a clear and no-nonsense message.

Think back to the last time you received a clear, concise e-mail. Wasn't it refreshing and easier to engage with?

You need to know that your boundaries are in your control. You have the ability to decide when and how to draw the line in your life. This will be one of the most empowering lessons you ever learn.

How to Picture a Boundary

Depending on your personality and outlook, you may think of a boundary as an encircling brick wall or perhaps a fresh-looking picket fence with a gate always propped open, but we'd like to invite you to also think of your personal boundary in quite a different way.

Consider human skin. It's dense enough to protect and contain us, but flexible enough to allow for movement. Skin is porous in the upper layers so what's necessary can pass through – sweat can be excreted and sunshine absorbed to help us make vitamin D. Skin is also sufficiently tough to withstand accidental damage, and it's capable of amazing re-growth.

As with skin, we can feel discomfort – even temporary pain at times – when boundaries get damaged either internally or from the outside when we don't take care. Yet, again like our skin, boundaries are amazing because they can grow with us.

Why have we chosen to use skin as a metaphor? Because skin keeps us in contact with others – it's not a brick wall or other type of opaque barrier. Studies show that skin-to-skin contact is actually vital for humans. Think of the studies which have shown that 'kangaroo care' – the nestling of a naked newborn on its parents' bare chests – improves outcomes in premature baby care. And equally our skin can act as an early warning system for our entire bodies. Think of how your skin prickles when another person gets too close – it's a very physical sensation.

Now, let's look at your own personal boundaries.

EXERCISE: Your Personal Boundary

You will need another person to do this exercise with you. This other should be a friend or colleague but not someone with whom you are very close. We understand this may not feel easy, and you would be more comfortable with someone more familiar to you. But in close relationships, boundaries will be well established. We need you to step outside your comfort zone in order to experience a fresh boundary.

Begin by standing facing each other a comfortable distance apart – this might be four foot away from each other, or more or less.

You are going to stay on your spot. Notice the distance that feels comfortable. Now ask your exercise partner to step closer. They are now in charge of their movements and are gradually going to take one step at a time towards you, pausing for 30 seconds between each step. In that pause, consider how comfortable you feel.

As they come closer, note when you start to feel some level of discomfort. And when do you notice you are really not happy, and that your skin is starting to throw up a few goosebumps? When do you want to scream 'stop' – because your personal space now feels properly invaded? At that point ask your partner to step back.

So, what just happened?

This is your body unconsciously registering where it feels most comfortable in relation to another person. This is your discernible physical boundary. Bear this in mind as you read through the book – who oversteps this boundary and who stays too far away?

At the end of this book you will find blank pages for you to write down your experience of exercises like this and ideas that you want to make a note of so you can build up your own Learning Journal as you work through the book.

Part of understanding how to use boundaries is learning to look at interpersonal relationships and your own part in them. Then, deciding where and how to establish a boundary doesn't just get easier, it becomes self-evident. The exercise above is your first step towards this.

Developing confidence in your own decision-making and its effect on your behaviour will make you happier as it means you are properly owning and taking care of yourself. In our experience: boundaries can give peace of mind. Boundaries give freedom. Boundaries are bliss.

STEP ONE:

ME, MYSELF, I

'The greatest discovery of all time is that a person can change his future by merely changing his attitude.'

OPRAH WINFREY

It is so important that you care for yourself first before you decide how much you can give to or care for another. Self-care is not selfish or even self-centred – quite the opposite. Remember when you get on a plane how the flight attendants tell you – in the case of emergency – to put on your own oxygen mask first, before helping others?

That's a practical example of self-care – which is clearly aimed at a wider good. Setting self-boundaries is not about ignoring the needs of others, it's about not ignoring yourself.

Take a minute to notice your reactions to what you have just read. What are your thoughts and feelings? When you read about the oxygen mask, does that make sense?

Can you think of a recent example of an occasion when you have put yourself first? Perhaps it was having an early night when others expected you to stay up to help or entertain them. Maybe you can't think of an example, but you may know someone who seems confident in putting their needs first (but whom you don't think of as selfish). You might view them as 'sorted' or 'in control'. Write these initial thoughts down in your Learning Journal.

In Step One, we will learn to create and/or strengthen our

personal boundaries which affect sleep, fitness, unhealthy habits, social media and e-mail and our attitude to our 'self' in general. We will also introduce a concept called the 'Drama Triangle', which explains how you interact with others.

In Jennie's clinical practice, many clients come with an array of real problems involving other people – such as spouses or children – but what is often underlying is a lack of self-care and a surprising lack of awareness of their own needs. Encouraging them to focus on themselves first makes it easier to tackle their issues with others.

We all benefit from a bit of time and space to reflect on our lives and ourselves. And this book isn't a replacement for therapy or suggesting anyone needs it. But Jennie knows from more than twenty years in practice – working all over the UK – there are many recurring personal and emotional issues which boundaries can help with.

Have you ever reflected on your personal rules for life – those that dictate things like our bedtimes, eating habits, manners and attitudes to relationships, which all develop over time. These are our 'self-boundaries' – and they primarily affect us (though they may well have a knock-on effect on others).

Here, we'll be exploring our key self-boundaries and explaining how we can set them, taking into account our practical and emotional needs. This is a holistic approach to life – getting into the habit of caring for ourself in all regards. Treating ourself with respect and kindness will change the way we live, before we even start improving relationships with those around us.

We're going to put you back in charge of your own life, before we go on to explaining how to use boundaries with others.

EXERCISE: Visualise Your Boundary*

Read through the following, then start.

Sitting in a comfy chair, take a few deep breaths and close your eyes. Settle yourself. Notice your breathing throughout the exercise.

Now, picture yourself stood in a large field. It is a beautiful sunny day, with blue sky, birds singing and lush green grass underfoot. Take a good look around your field and notice where you are in the field.

As you stand there, imagine that a boundary appears around you. What does it look like? What is it made of? How wide is it? How tall? Is it the same all the way around? Are there doors or windows? How do you feel within your boundary?

Now, imagine your field is becoming populated first with your family, then friends, then work colleagues, and finally everyone in your life, some closer, some further away. The boundary stays in place, but some may be within it and some outside.

Note again how you feel inside your boundary. Who is near to you, and who is far away?

Then open your eyes.

Go to your Learning Journal and answer these questions (you may want to draw rather than write your response): What does your boundary look like? Can you describe it? How did you feel when you were inside it? Did you feel safe, trapped, or lonely? Was there a difference between how you felt when there was and wasn't a boundary? What was it like when the other people appeared in your field? What's your view on your boundary? Does it feel secure? Does it allow you to be in contact with others or is it too rigid?

---

* Listen to this visualisation exercise for free on Soundcloud at bit.ly/visualise-your-boundary

Are you surprised at your responses? Looking back at this bound-ary, would you consider it to be good enough? If not, write down what that 'perfect' boundary might look like. For example, if the boundary that first came into your mind had a perimeter of barbed wire, would you prefer it to be a natural, more porous hedge? It's useful to do this exercise and imagine a physical boundary, but don't worry – this mental picture can and will change as you become more confident of your needs.

So, why do your own boundaries matter in the context of others' behaviour? Let's consider Robinson Crusoe, Daniel Defoe's famous castaway, who chose to live to a routine that helped him – in his own words – 'stay sane'. With no one around him to impose boundaries, rules, or expectations on him, his survival – and happi-ness – depended on him making and keeping promises to himself in terms of behaviour.

But how would anyone fare on a desert island with no self-rules? Think of an alternative destination: the location in *Lord of the Flies*, William Golding's novel of 1954. In this book, a group of young boys are marooned on an island and must find their own way in order to survive. One of the older boys, Piggy, appeals to reason, 'Which is better – to have rules and agree, or to hunt and kill? . . . law and rescue, or hunting and breaking things up?' But the other children – who don't display any personal boundaries – do not know how to control their impulses, and soon individual lives and the group's salvation are threatened.

Which island would you rather live on? One which is governed by good sense, responsible behaviour and self-care or the other, which has the false attraction of there being no boundaries? This feels like the ultimate freedom, but descends in time to anarchy and survival of the fittest.

EXERCISE: The Debating Table

In this exercise, we are going to show you how to identify their 'self'. Our inner voice or sense of self is multi-faceted. Everyone has competing thoughts, feelings and beliefs which influence their conscious choices; you will have been accumulating these (often without knowing) since birth. Some we take heed of more than others. This exercise is about learning to listen to your whole 'self' before you make a decision – not just the voices that shout loudest.

Picture yourself sitting at a favourite table where you might reasonably have a work discussion or family debate. This could be in a boardroom, a kitchen, or even outside in your garden. You are sitting at the head of the table. This is you at your most composed – you are aware of all that is around you, thinking and feeling with conscious good intent.

As an example, we're going to explore what would happen in the case of a holiday windfall.

You are handed a piece of paper that says that you have won £1,000 to spend on a holiday but you have to decide where you are going within the next hour or the offer will expire.

As you look up from this piece of paper, the table has become populated with others who feel familiar to you. They sit down on all sides and begin to discuss the offer.

Notice that there is a child at the table bouncing up and down and saying, 'Can we go to the beach, can we go to the beach?' You feel an excitement in yourself at this response. When was the last time you went to the sea and had a beach holiday? That would be great, you think.

But then a stern voice coming from an older person than yourself sat at the other side of the table says, 'Well, that sounds a frivolous waste of money. We should put it to good use and go on a cultural trip – I vote for a coach drive across Europe. Think of all the cities we could pack in.'

As the chair of the discussion, you notice the disappointment of the child whose shoulders droop.

'Driving for hours? Yuck,' they retort.

To you, the idea of the drive is appealing and yes, it would be a good use of the money you think, but you notice that you don't feel as excited as at the beach holiday idea.

The older person is talking again: 'This is a lot of money and shouldn't be wasted on a beach holiday, this is for the grown-ups to decide.'

Again, you clock the disappointed expression of the child.

But now you notice another child sat very quietly, hands in their lap, looking around at everyone: 'Please may I say something?' they say as they put their hand up. You nod encouragement.

They continue, 'Well, I would like to go on the drive. I know it would be good for me and make everyone else happy.' The older one nods with approval and the child goes slightly pink with pleasure at this acknowledgement.

The child who wanted to go to the beach bursts into tears. At their shoulder, another child appears and bangs their fists on the table, shouting, 'It's not fair, you never listen to me,' while glaring at the older person.

A soothing voice floats across the table; another older person has appeared. 'There, there. We will listen to you but not while you are shouting. I like the idea of both holidays but maybe we could find another solution. This shouldn't be just for us. Who else can we take? I know that Uncle Theo hasn't had a holiday for ages, so I vote for a city break near a beach and we take Uncle Theo.'

The quiet child's response: 'I agree.'

The shouty child's response: 'Yuck, I hate Uncle Theo! He smells.'

The beach child's response: 'No, thanks. I still vote for beach.'

The first older person's response: 'We will decide what's best; it's not a decision for children.'

The second older person's response: 'Well, we need to find a solution that's nice for all of us.'

All eyes turn and look at you. 'What shall we do?' they say in unison.

Now, think about what you would do in this scenario. What would be your decision? And who has the loudest voice at your table, because this is a metaphor for you and the different 'selves' you are made up from.

Now draw your debating table in the Learning Journal section.

Some of these 'selves' — happy, demanding, thoughtful, pleasing, controlling — will be more familiar to you than others. Notice that some of the voices — the happy, cross, eager-to-please selves — are like children while the controlling and organising voices remind us of the older people who have influenced us, such as parents, grandparents, teachers, uncles, aunts, nannies, older siblings and anyone in authority. This is because our feelings, thoughts and behaviours are shaped — consciously and unconsciously — when we are children looking to our parents (or those in an influential role). Think about who you have identified as someone who would be around your table.

We'll be referring to some feelings, thoughts, or behaviours as 'Child-like' or 'Parental' from now on, and also to those moments when you are being your most authentic self as 'Adult'. These Adult moments are when you chair meetings at this table and make decisions based on all available evidence presented to you at this time.

Think of this as your personal debating table; the voices are the various aspects of you. None are superior in status whatever they say – all need to be heard.

Draw the Line: *a healthy self-boundary means taking all of those voices into consideration, but the Adult makes the decision.*

Transactional Analysis

The terms 'Parent', 'Adult' and 'Child' are used in a model of psycho-therapy, counselling, education and organisation called Transactional Analysis, which is the basis for the exercises given in this book. You don't need to study TA to use and benefit from this book but we have included an appendix at the back which goes into the theory in more detail for anyone interested in learning more (see page 289).

And the answer to the holiday dilemma? Your Adult self, with healthy boundaries in place, would book that beach holiday with some culture thrown in and leave Uncle Theo at home. Did you reach this conclusion? And if not, which strong voices led you to another decision? Make a note in your Learning Journal as to which voices you listened to more around the debating table.

Hold your debating table in mind as you work through this book. You will need it when considering other situations and problems.

Let's Get Started

In this section, let's look at the self-boundaries (or lack of them) you have and show you how to set new ones. It may feel uncomfortable and even strange to begin with. This is because our heads buzz with decision-making all day long, being pulled between the demands of our inner voices (Parent or Child) we have just introduced you to. Meanwhile, our emotions are also on constant alert, creating feelings which need to be assessed before we respond to them.

Draw the Line: *remember that self-boundaries are personal to us – like our own skin – which, in order to be in peak condition, needs care and nourishment. The more confidence you develop in your own decision-making and first-class self-care you give to yourself, the more that your self-boundary (or skin) will glow.*

A good example of someone with healthy self-boundaries is Mary Poppins – she is comfortable being 'practically perfect in every way' (said without self-deprecation), administers her own medicine without complaint, is charmed by her chimney sweep Bert but not bowled over and knows when to leave the family to care for itself (because her work is done).

Think again of that debating table of competing voices all trying to win the holiday argument. A healthy self-boundary will help you manage those voices – while also listening to them, and drawing from any wisdom on offer. Someone used to setting and maintaining good self-boundaries knows they can hear all points of view but they are confident when making the final decision.

EXERCISE: Getting to Know You

This exercise is about reflecting on and understanding the different parts of yourself.

Think back over the past week:

Can you identify one or more occasions when you have cared for yourself or taken time to have a moment to yourself? Perhaps you enjoyed a bath or took the dog out on your own.

Can you think of one occasion when you have criticised or felt disappointed in yourself? Something like, 'I went for a run but I didn't try hard enough/should have done better.'

Can you identify an occasion when you have cared for another? You might have offered a cup of tea to a tired co-worker.

Can you remember an occasion when you criticised someone else (either out loud or to yourself)? Perhaps you moaned about a co-worker for being always tired.

Have you noticed a thought about something – say, a newspaper article – that on reflection owes more to your parents' ideas than what you know you feel? Something like: 'Isn't the Royal Family marvellous?'

Have you enjoyed a spontaneous moment with friends? Did you laugh at a ridiculous situation?

Have you felt frightened but known this to be irrational? For example, if waking up from a nightmare and feeling too scared to sleep again.

Have you sulked or deliberately provoked a fight? Did you take out a bad mood on a partner?

Have you been consciously pleasing to another? You might have offered compliments to cheer someone up.

Looking back at the week – how was your time divided up? Do you spend more hours overall being critical either of yourself or others, or do you spend quite a lot of time caring for yourself or others? How often do you aim to please others, and how frequently do you enjoy moments of spontaneous fun?

Now, think about which of these experiences or feelings correlate most closely to the Parental or Child-like voices at your debating table. Be aware that this is a matter of personal degree.

Remember that no single viewpoint is superior in some way. Simply, you are making observations not judgements to help you analyse your own behaviour, thoughts and feelings. You have taken the first steps into a deepening of the understanding you have of yourself. Use your Learning Journal space to make notes.

In the next part of this Step, we are going to introduce you to some key areas where you can begin to introduce new boundaries into your day-to-day life. These will have practical benefits for your relationships, happiness and health, as well as teaching you the basics of boundary-making.

Sleep

We'd like you to look at establishing good self-boundaries around sleep first. We start with sleep as these self-boundaries will put you in a much healthier, more relaxed and mentally stronger place to decide what you want for yourself and from others.

When we don't have enough sleep, the competing voices in our head are louder and harder to analyse; think how difficult it is to make a decision if you are overtired and how easy it is to overreact emotionally to situations you might otherwise shrug off. We're sure you can think of a problem that seemed to solve itself or diminish after a good night's sleep.

BRING IN THE BOUNDARIES:

Your Sleep Plan

How well do you sleep? Are you resigned to your sleep pattern or constantly in a state of stress about it? Perhaps you recognise one or more of these sleep issues: the struggle to drop off, intermittent sleeping, waking up tired, waking up too early, wanting to sleep during the day, or needing to catch up at weekends? Whatever the issue, a new sleep self-boundary will be of huge benefit. So, let's start.

Set your own perfect bedtime. Start by keeping a sleep diary and note each evening when you start to feel properly tired, not just a weary sensation. We mean the type of tiredness that means you will fall asleep quickly. As you set your sleep boundary, this feeling may take a few weeks to become recognisable, and your proper time to fall asleep may be earlier or later than you believed or wanted.

Once you have clocked this ideal go-to-sleep time, work backwards from it to establish a bedtime. How long does it take to lock up, put the cat out and turn the dishwasher on? How long for teeth cleaning, etc.? What's an ideal reading time if you enjoy a book in bed or want to make time for sex?

So, the night-time ritual might read: 10 p.m. – put the dishwasher on, check the front door; 10.15 p.m. – clean teeth, check on children; 10.30 p.m. – in bed; 11 p.m. – fall asleep.

Note that this doesn't include time for gadgets in bed – even podcasts or your favourite TV show. Electrical devices need to be banned from the bedroom. Notice your response to this ban; part of you probably doesn't like this idea. It may be your inner child wanting its toys, but the Adult you knows that toys don't help you sleep well. You might use TV or late-night music as a form of comfort to help you drop off – even though you often wake later if the programme changes abruptly or switches off. Another little voice in your head may be warning that you will feel worse if you try to stop this habit, as it acknowledges that you have become reliant on audio-visual stimulation. Perhaps this means you don't ever get through REM sleep – the light dreamlike state – into the deep sleep state where the body starts repairing itself.

So, what can you do at bedtime? The simple answer is sleep, sex and reading – as long as you don't end up more awake. With reading in mind, any subject matter is fine but it must not be work-related, or disturbing, or depressing. You can use a Kindle-like device if the illumination is adjusted so your retinas are not being exposed to blue – or daylight-type – light, which is known to affect sleep patterns.

It's ideal to keep the same sleep routine seven days a week, so this means no super-late weekend lie-ins. An exception might be if you may have to get up early for work at a time you know is not ideal for yourself. Allow yourself to sleep later on non-work days, but don't exceed a normal, healthy eight hours.

Some people experience waking in the night. When this happens, we have little reasoning available to us at that time, which is why we may feel anxious or frightened (like a Child). Or we may become self-critical – going over our day and all the things we got wrong or berating ourselves for what we haven't done (as a Parent might). In the bright light of day, we know this isn't helpful but at night we feel marooned in our fear. So, what to do?

Soothing yourself back to sleep

Waking up in the night is especially tough. Here's how to get back to sleep again – by soothing yourself.

First, take the stress out of trying to get to sleep by realising that simply resting in itself is good. Are there only two hours of sleep before you get up? Reframe that: that's a whole two hours of rest you will be having.

Second, be kind to yourself. Notice that you are warm, comfortable and can relax and rest. In doing that you may realise that you are too hot/cold. Open a window, have a fresh pillow by your bed that will be cool, or have a blanket by your bed to warm yourself up.

Some are familiar with the practice of giving yourself a hard time emotionally at night: 'I should have done a better job yesterday;

I shouldn't have snapped at my partner.' Rather than speaking like a cross Parent to yourself, purposefully move to being nurturing – 'Come on, now is not the time to be thinking these things.' And make the tone gentle, as if you were talking to an anxious child: 'Rest now and tomorrow it can be sorted out.' This really isn't the time to be dealing with problems.

You may also feel nervous or scared: 'What if my partner hates me for what I said earlier? Am I useless at my job? What's that noise?' Again, be kind and tell yourself: 'Come on, it's OK. I can sort this out tomorrow, now is not the time to be fretting.'

The revolving bedroom door

What if your sleep is affected by others – be they nomadic children, pets on the bed, or a duvet-snatching partner? How can your self-boundaries manage the behaviour of others?

What parent doesn't know the patter of small sleepy feet when your child is coming in for a midnight cuddle, story, glass of water, or other excuse to see Mummy and Daddy?

Keeping your child out of your bed may be a tough self-boundary as you respond to an almost primeval need to protect the young. But caveman parents didn't have to set an alarm, get children to school, commute to an office and then spend a day full of reports, meetings and office politics. You don't have the luxury of time, however, you do have the greater luxury of safety. You don't need to be on high alert 24/7 to protect your child from hungry bears.

Ask yourself if you need to be either in the same room as your child, or sleeping with one ear open in case they need you to pay a visit to them. Stand back and look at 365 days a year. Realistically, how often is a child going to need you in the night? Unless they have a chronic condition or a serious illness, the chances are that it will be just a handful of nights. Yet many parents feel and behave as though the call could come at any time every night. Notice the difference between reality and fantasy. Think, too, how much better it would be for the whole family if – should illness occur – a parent is already rested.

We're going to look at sleep boundaries for children later on in the book. For now, though, the key to keeping children in their own beds is consistency. When a child invader comes in, be calm and reassuring as you take them back to their bed firmly but with kindness. Be consistent in your parenting and do give it time. A few weeks at least to re-establish good habits for all the family. Be patient and remember that it wouldn't be fair to your child to break the new boundary and let them sleep in your bed one night a week or when your partner's away. Note your reaction to this – are you feeling defensive?

Do notice the first time you get a good night's sleep and con-gratulate yourself on establishing a well-held boundary. Some are tougher than others to put in place.

But children are not the only nocturnal visitors or additional bed guests. You may feel that the comfort you get from allowing a trusted pet companion to share your sleeping space helps you to nod off. But, if you are having sleepless nights, Fido may be to blame.

Vets warn that animal nocturnal behaviour is not compatible with the human sleep cycle – cats, for example, may wake you in the small hours for food or company as this suits their natural biorhythms. Interestingly, dogs may see the bed as their territory and push you to the edges as they stretch, scratch and snore. Your dog here is the one with the strong self-boundary as he or she has claimed the territory of the bed as their own and is defending it to the detriment of your sleep. How often have we heard pet owners 'jokingly' recount nights spent curled up at the edge of the bed while their Alsatian stretches out in luxury? They may then shrug and say, 'What can you do? I wouldn't be able to sleep without him.'

If this is you, put the question of pets in your bed to your internal debating table. Which is the loudest voice at the table? Is it the Parental part of you, which has turned Fido into a substitute or additional child and worries about him feeling neglected or lonely if kept in another room? Is it your rebellious voice – maybe responsible for that defensive feeling mentioned earlier – saying, 'My parents wouldn't let me have a pet, so I am going to love this one however I choose and break all their rules'? Or, is it your anxious Child, who wants both the comfort of the living cuddly toy and the protection the dog represents against potential burglars or even monsters in the night?

Listen to the voices but now challenge what they are saying. If Fido is there for comfort, but you are not sleeping well, how much good is that doing you? If you are sleeping eight good hours a night, that comfort would not be so necessary.

Draw the Line: *good self-care doesn't equal self-spoiling. It's not about indulging yourself but taking mature decisions.*

We're going to assume that a mature dog or cat or a young animal can be trained. First, create a comfy sleeping area for them in a separate room well away from your own bedroom. Be consistent with not allowing them to sleep anywhere else. If they try to join you, cry or chew, be calm and reassuring but don't give in. As with re-training children at night, do give it time. Be persistent and consistent. If this isn't enough, you may want to bring in a dog behaviourist to help.

Or is it your beloved keeping you awake? This may be through sleep talking, snoring, restlessness, duvet-hogging, hot flushes, early starts, or late nights. It may not be a new problem – but just because their sleeping behaviour is entrenched in your family bed there is no reason to put up with its consequences. All these problems have a root cause so that's where you'll find your sleep solution.

Sleep talking: if this is the problem, don't wake them up when it is happening. Reassure them in their sleep that everything is OK. Sleep talking is often the result of an anxious brain processing during the night. Talk to them about what might be troubling them and suggest that they write down their worries before they go to sleep. Through talking they may realise there is a problem to address, and want to get some outside help.

Persistent snoring: this needs a chat with the GP to assess physical symptoms as snoring can be a sign of sleep apnoea and other breathing difficulties. A doctor may suggest lifestyle changes such as weight loss or interventions including day surgery. Perhaps this sounds like something which might lead to a row, with the non-snorer suffering guilt and the snorer feeling shame and resentment? But there is nothing wrong with caring for yourself and others, and this is a classic example of such a moment. By encouraging your snoring partner to seek help, you could well be encouraging them to make a dramatic improvement to their health overall. The peace at night is a beneficial by-product to the relationship as a whole – and who could argue with that?

Restlessness: this can be caused by lifestyle issues such as caffeine consumption, not enough exercise, weight issues, or too much alcohol. This is a good example of where your self-boundaries can be weakened by someone else's lack of boundaries. We'll come back to this later in the book, but for now ask your partner what they can do to improve any/all of these areas.

Duvet hogging: get two duvets.

Hot flushes (for you and/or your partner): having your own duvet will help. A fan is useful, as is bedding made of natural fibres, including silk. Talk to your GP about natural ways to support the menopause and discuss whether hormone replacement therapy (HRT) might be right for you or your partner.

Early starts or late nights: shift work can take a toll on many relationships because it does disturb everyone's sleep. Simple tricks like leaving clothes for the next day in another room and minimising all chances of disruption can help. Sleep masks can be useful too. Conversations and mutual consideration are key.

> **Draw the Line:** *self-boundaries don't just mean being firm with ourselves, but with others. Sometimes the greatest threat to you building a strong set of self-boundaries comes from the person you love most.*

You'll notice how in order to achieve your sleep self-boundary in a situation where you share your bed, your co-sleeper will have to put some boundaries in place too. Whether this means addressing their own health, their attitude to bedtime, or talking about their feelings more, your partner's self-boundary is linked to yours. Throughout the book, there will be examples of this and sometimes you will find this challenging. Our self-boundaries are crucial to our personal wellbeing but they will have an effect on those closest to us. This is not a reason to give up as the case history on fitness in the next section shows.

EXERCISE: Simple Body Scan*

Trouble getting to sleep or maybe you suffer from 3 a.m. wakeful-ness? With time, this will help you to relax and head off to the Land of Nod.

Practice this during the day when you can be on your own and not disturbed. Either lying in your bed or on a sofa, take a few breaths, settle yourself and close your eyes.

Now imagine a light above your body. It can be any colour you find comforting – white, lilac, gold – and it can be warm or cool as suits your surroundings and mood.

Start at your toes and visualise the light moving slowly up to your head and back down again, relaxing each muscle as you go. As it shines on different parts of your body, mentally and physically relax the muscles there.

Allow yourself to sink into the bed and breathe slowly and deeply as you drift into sleep.

Setting your sleep boundaries will start a virtuous circle. Engaging that considered voice – which has listened to all your internal opinions – when considering self-boundaries will help you to rest. Being more rested will allow you to engage that voice again when you need to review another self-boundary. Overall, be kind to yourself and know that rest is good. Take the pressure off.

Now go to your Learning Journal pages and note the sleep self-boundaries you can start to work on.

---

* Listen to this visualisation exercise for free on Soundcloud at bit.ly/visualise-your-boundary

Fitness

In this section, we'll introduce the self-boundaries you need to implement around exercise.

Ask yourself this: what was your reaction to reading the section sub-heading 'Fitness'? Did you want to skip this section? Perhaps you thought you didn't need to read it, or were afraid – not just of what it might say but how it might make you feel?

Write this feeling down. Which inner voice is talking, do you think? Perhaps it is a lofty, 'I don't need this,' which sounds a bit like a Parent talking. Or maybe, 'This feels exciting; I love running around,' which is like a Child. An Adult response would be 'I wonder what I can learn from this,' however experienced or motivated you already are.

We're all aware these days of how vital it is to get and maintain fitness. Numerous studies have shown the benefits of regular exercise for cardiovascular and mental health. But, how do you draw the line between managing your body for optimum, age-related health and becoming either too overwhelmed to start or too obsessed to stop? Those who develop a fanatical approach to fitness have self-boundaries which are just as weak as those who do no sport. The healthy position lies between the two and is the one that comes with positive self-boundaries – knowing how much and how often to exercise so that your fitness will improve but not dominate your life and relationships.

First, decide how fit you need to be to care for yourself. We would advise visiting your GP practice before taking up a new exercise regime, especially if you are aged over 50. That may mean blood pressure, cholesterol and blood sugar level testing. You may consider yourself to be in good shape but don't take that for granted. Inherited cholesterol issues affect slim people as well as those who are heavier; and doctors have also warned about the development of internal fat around organs, which is believed to be more dangerous for your health than a little extra visible fat on your thighs.

You could use a gym to have an assessment with a personal trainer. You may prefer to use a monitoring wristband – like a Fitbit or Nike+ FuelBand. Or you could check your BMI against NHS guidelines – and at the same time, count your daily steps to see how close they are to the recommended daily 10,000. You could also try timing how long it takes to walk to a set point. These tests and measures will give you a practical idea of how fit you are and what you might want to do, but some people will still find it difficult to build and maintain a self-boundary around fitness.

BRING IN THE BOUNDARIES:

Your Fitness Plan

Whatever your current state – couch potato or marathon runner – here are some ways to improve your self-boundary towards a healthier state of fitness.

Take the Adult position and say, 'What can I learn that might make a difference to me?'

Note down three things you might like to change. These could be: 'I just want to get off the sofa'; 'I don't want to let fitness run my life'; or 'I want to get moving for the sake of my aching back or stiff joints'.

Getting your body into a healthy condition can be done in lots of ways. Gyms and running are not for everyone – nor do they have to be. Not all fitness has to be competitive either. If you find sport intimidating for that reason, perhaps you might consider Tai Chi or something in a group, like line dancing. Think of a long-lost passion – such as horse riding – could you do that again? Get out of the mindset that fitness has to look a certain way and/or equal slog.

How much time can you give to fitness weekly? Whatever you choose needs to fit in with the time available, rather than you squeezing a busy schedule tighter – which will give you an excuse to fail.

The same can be true for cost and/or facilities. If you live miles from a town, don't pressure yourself to join a gym you may find hard to visit. The answer might lie in a pedometer.

Draw the Line: *set yourself up for success, not failure. But if you do step backwards, don't give up hope. The boundary is still in place, it just needs a little more attention.*

Buddy systems have their uses, but a self-boundary isn't one you can share. If your buddy falls by the wayside, it can be difficult not to follow suit. Enjoy company if it helps with your motivation, but don't let it be your only motivation.

At all times be wary of following in other people's footsteps, particularly your parents' or those of other important individuals in your life. If you instinctively don't want to do a type of exercise, ask yourself why. Did your mum, dad, or sibling do it so well that you feel you can never compete? In which case, understand that you don't have to do this to participate at their level – you can just be yourself and enjoy it.

Self-boundaries can be challenged by our relationships with our emotional partners; however, they are not the only threats to our self-care. The challenge could equally well come from parents, friends, or children, even if they don't realise they are affecting our personal decisions.

CASE HISTORY

This example highlights the impact those around us have on our boundaries: Liam and Grace came to Jennie's practice together with a familiar problem of miscommunication. But as Jennie began to work with them, one issue popped up which turned out to be quite typical of their relationship. They seemed unable to create secure healthy self-boundaries which didn't leave the other person feeling excluded. Both were so focused on 'caring' for their relationship, they had no time or mental space to 'care' for themselves.

The couple explained to Jennie that every New Year's resolution for the past half-decade would be to join the local gym and get fit. Both had a history of type 2 diabetes in the family, and as they approached middle age, they were keen to avoid that illness, and indeed any others. Both regularly moaned to each other about thickening waistlines and feeling a bit sluggish.

But when the local gym had a membership offer, Liam – frustrated by Grace's procrastination – had filled in a form for himself (self-care in action), leaving her form on the kitchen table.

Liam told Jennie he felt guilty, although he also felt really motivated to take action. Grace meanwhile said she felt let down and left behind. She was so cross she could hardly look at Liam as she talked, even though this seemed at first sight to be quite a minor incident.

Liam did offer up that he felt bad every time he went to the gym but his drive to get fit was overriding. There were moments of doubt of course, particularly when he came home tired from work and Grace was already sipping wine in front of a new box set. He told Jennie he was torn between flopping down next to her, but wanting to honour his commitment to a new kickboxing class.

As he talked, Grace started looking sulky and withdrawn. Here, Liam was caught between setting a clear self-boundary for himself regarding fitness and his desire to please his partner. Neither could see how to resolve this.

Jennie began by asking them to reflect back to that scene – and to look at what was happening with their thoughts and feelings. She was using the debating table technique.

Liam said his thoughts and feelings were as follows:

- *A pull to join Grace on the sofa – 'It's more important to have harmony in the home and a happy Grace than going to the gym; I can get fit some other time.'*
- *'I could sit on the sofa to please her; bringing crisps and more wine.'*
- *'I'm feeling insecure – are we drifting apart?'*
- *'I want to start nagging Grace to join me. If I persist long enough, surely she will get off the sofa?'*
- *One quieter voice at the table wanted to express a more frustrated opinion – that of a rebellious child: 'I want to storm out – I feel undermined and angry.'*

Grace listened and responded with the feelings and thoughts present at her own internal debating table:

- *'Why doesn't Liam want us to be happy the way we always were? What's changed?'*

- *'I'm feeling insecure – is this behaviour driven by something or someone outside the home?'*
- *'Is he going to get fit and not want me anymore?'*
- *'Why should I go at his pace? I'll go when I'm ready.'* That is Grace's rebellious inner child talking.
- *'It's too late, he'll already be so much fitter. I can't catch up.'*
- *'He's irresponsible – we can't afford this.'*
- *'He's selfish – because he's spending our money without consultation.'*

And underlying all of these:

- *'I'm scared. I feel very frightened at the thought of walking into a gym, and above all else, I have a bigger fear of losing Liam.'*

So how did Jennie advise the couple to find their way through all this emotional confusion and internalised chaos and start down the road to better self-care?

Having done the debating table exercise, Jennie asked them to listen to all their competing voices in this scenario and work out what each was trying to say, before making a decision about how to act.

Jennie unpicked some of their comments. She pointed out that Liam's urge to join Grace and abandon his own exercise isn't as kind as it sounds. This sort of care is colluding with the problem. Both would end up not going to the gym – and not forming a self-boundary around fitness – which ultimately would be the worst decision. Jennie noted none of his responses seemed to have been made in a considered here-and-now way. She commented that it would appear that his weak self-boundary put him at the mercy of his and Grace's feelings and thoughts, buffeted about and feeling frustrated as a result.

Taking into account Grace's feelings and thoughts, Jennie observed that there was little headspace here for thoughtful and reasoned decision-making. No wonder both were becoming entrenched in their positions.

This feeling of being stuck between a rock and a hard place with no other options is your alarm call that boundaries are missing or about to be breached, and a pause button is needed. In pressing that button, you will gain breathing space to assess your thoughts and feelings and become aware there are always more options. There is a way out.

So with Liam and Grace, Jennie explained that they needed to set and keep to clear self-boundaries around their own behaviour, and stop expecting the other to change and match them. That they needed to be more open about their thoughts and feelings, and stop expecting the other to mind-read, a common theme with couples.

Liam and Grace agreed to take a fresh look at the situation and map out a way they could resolve this together by accepting they had other mutual beneficial options.

Draw the Line: *in any situation where you are trying to renew or develop self-boundaries, you need to make a plan. Be aware that the greatest pressure on you may well come from those closest to you because love can soften any boundary.*

Liam and Grace's plan looked like this:

Step 1: Liam sits down and asks for the TV to be turned off for five minutes.

Step 2: Liam states he is feeling uncomfortable about going to the gym but knows for his health he must maintain the routine.

Step 3: Grace authentically responds about how she is genuinely feeling. This means revealing she feels scared – and talking about her feelings rather than criticising Liam.

Step 4: This opens up a dialogue between them as to what is happening in the here and now.

Step 5: In understanding each other Liam still goes to the gym, but having assuaged her concerns, Grace agrees to accompany him the next time or she decides the gym isn't for her, but agrees that it is right for him.

This is based on a conclusion that Liam going to the gym is to both their benefits; keeping Liam healthy will mean Grace doesn't face the prospect of supporting or nursing him through chronic illness in later life. Meanwhile Liam can be supportive over Grace's concerns about fitness but ultimately, she must make her own decision, and set her own self-boundary. That could look like Liam working out at the gym three times a week, and Grace deciding to swim at the local pool during two lunchtimes each week.

They both accept that this means slight timetable changes at home but have established fitness boundaries that are likely to last, based as they are on each individual's own reasonable expectations and self-care, not the demands of others.

Draw the Line: *bear in mind every boundary you bolster through reading this book will have a knock-on effect on another boundary, possibly one belonging to someone else.*

Having just worked through an example of setting self-care boundaries around fitness, you will find that the same approach works for any boundary you are concerned about: examine the problem using the debating table, analyse where you can make changes, set a plan and execute it.

Before you move on, turn to your Learning Journal pages, and start your own plan for your fitness self-boundaries.

Eating Habits

The self-boundary around what and how we eat – like those around fitness and sleep – is utterly essential for our physical and mental wellbeing. Yet it is a line many people find increasingly difficult to draw.

If you found the section subheading 'Fitness' not to your taste, the chances are you will have also felt a strong reaction to seeing the words 'eating habits' – perhaps even a judgemental one.

Now is not the time to be swayed off-course. Your dietary needs are important as being well-fuelled is not just an end in itself, it's vital to establishing all your self-boundaries. Food for human beings is not an option or a luxury.

First, let's make it plain that when we talk about eating habits we don't just mean a diet to shed weight. We're talking about a lifelong healthy attitude towards food and drink, which nourishes as well as pleases.

So what is your initial reaction to food? Tick any of these which apply:

'I should be on a slimming diet, I shouldn't eat sugar, I shouldn't eat meat, I shouldn't eat bread.'

- 'I shouldn't eat on the run, I should eat at a table.'
- 'It's my job to feed everyone else. I believe I am always having to cook even if I'm not hungry. I like to feed others.'
- 'Men need to eat large portions of meat to stay strong.'
- 'I eat a sandwich at my desk because that's my workplace culture.'
- 'I need to stop and eat. I must have three courses.'
- 'I like keeping chocolate in the house as it tests my willpower and I feel good when others eat it and I don't.'
- 'I never allow myself what I would really like – a sticky bun. I'm an expert at counting calories.'
- 'I've done every diet. None work.'
- 'I don't like it but I notice what other people eat, and I can't seem to stop myself judging them in my head.'

Note any you recognise or endorse. Do they sound a little bossy or authoritative?

Other reactions might be more emotional, child-like, compliant, or rebellious:

- 'I have to eat everything on my plate, I have to have pudding. I need to eat at a certain time. Food is comforting, soothing and/or rewarding.'
- 'One biscuit isn't enough. No one will know if I eat more, it's my naughty secret.'
- 'I only feel OK if I have chocolate.'
- 'I don't like to eat in front of other people.'
- 'I feel good empty.'
- 'I feel good full.'
- 'I'll happily swap calories in food for calories in alcohol.'
- 'I toy with my food.'

- 'I believe I have food intolerances.'
- 'I get angry if I can't get what I want to eat or when I want to eat.'
- 'Nothing tastes as good as skinny feels.'
- 'I will eat what I like and hang the consequences.'

You may have felt any or all of these at some time. So, how can you shift into an Adult, boundaried approach to eating?

BRING IN THE BOUNDARIES:

Your Eating Habits Plan

We're now going to show you how to make a plan around your eating so you can establish those dietary self-boundaries.

First, ask yourself what statements did you agree with from the examples above? It is likely you will have reacted strongly to one set or the other.

The first set – the Parental-type authoritative or judgemental messages – included: 'you should do this', 'it's bad to eat like that'. The second set are more emotional child-like messages: 'I have to eat it all up', 'one biscuit isn't enough'. Or you may be assailed by a mixture of the two. Let's look at how you can break the cycle of messages and establish a new healthy self-boundary for each of your possible responses.

If you agree with the parental-type messages

First, acknowledge the problem. You may have already realised you cannot ignore those messages. Develop a mantra to use when you hear those voices. For example, 'I hear you but that's really not useful to me right now'.

Admit the history of your habit. You may have been eating according to guidelines put in place 30 years ago (e.g., always eat your potatoes first, never eat meat on a Friday). But you can acknowledge that the habit is not relevant for you now and it is time to change. You can take a decision that is right for you today, not as a response to those past messages/beliefs.

We'd like you to think of some strategies and note them down in your Learning Journal pages; these prompts will help you start:

- Do you know the difference between feeling hungry and thirsty?
- Focus on yourself and not what other people are eating.
- Stop fixating on your own food choices.
- Let others do the cooking; step back at least once a week.
- Having examined your own behaviour, what three small changes could you put in place? Write these down. Now, make a plan of who or what is most likely to sabotage your updated eating habits and how you could stop them breaching your new self-boundaries. Note down every week in your Learning Journal how you feel. Don't forget it takes a month to change a habit so be patient but consistent.

EXERCISE: Reset the Work Lunch

Did you nod in agreement at 'I eat at my desk/on the run'? If so, you may be thinking: what's wrong with that? I can keep working, and my boss sees how committed I am. Or if you are the boss, your employees can see how seriously you take your job.

But consider, where is the enjoyment in what you are eating, or pleasure in having a break? Eating while working will involve gulping down your food – you may not feel full, you may eat for longer than you need, or you may suffer indigestion. You also risk not monitoring how you are feeling as you eat so may well eat more or less than you think.

You are certainly denying yourself a natural break in the day. Is it really your boss's and co-workers' expectations that you should eat at your desk every day or are you buying into an unhealthy work culture? Rather than your boss respecting you for your devotion, they may see you as a bit of a doormat – and what happens to doormats? They get walked on.

Draw the Line: *don't let fear or embarrassment get in the way of caring for yourself. You cannot support others until your own foundations are truly secure.*

Acknowledge that you are not caring for yourself either physically or practically in terms of your career with this action. Note that it will feel uncomfortable to change this behaviour. It is going to take a while to feel OK.

Week One: make a contract with yourself. For the first five days, decide to leave your desk for 30 minutes at lunchtime – and set the time you will do this. It might be 12.30 p.m., 1 p.m., or 1.30 p.m. depending on what suits your work. You need to get up and walk away from your desk, taking your lunch with you, or going to another place like the canteen, a local café, or a bench in the park. Accept that you will feel uncomfortable but that sensation will change as you persist.

Week Two: it may have been a bit bumpy (people might have wondered where you were, phones may have gone unanswered, but the world of work has not fallen apart) so now you need to firm up that boundary – and give yourself 60 minutes. It may help to note the benefits at this point: you get to recharge your batteries, you talk to different work colleagues in the canteen, you notice you no longer get heartburn in the afternoon, you see other colleagues develop the confidence to do the same, and you realise your boss may respect you more.

Week Three: walking to get your lunch is becoming part of your fitness regime. You concentrate on what you eat and therefore take a healthier portion. You may find yourself losing weight and sleeping better. Your self-boundaries are working in harmony and supporting each other.

Bear in mind for this to be maintained long term, it has to be within the parameters of reality. You know what your job demands and when the busy periods are. If you're in a customer-facing position, your lunch may have to come at 2 p.m. or even 3 p.m., but it can still be a ring-fenced time and a much-needed break.

Week Four: make sure you notice the longer-term positives. These might be: better-quality lunches, improved relations with colleagues, a feeling of freshness in the afternoon and a renewed enthusiasm towards your job.

If you agree with the Child-like messages

If your dominant messaging around food is Child-like, how can you begin to eat in a more Adult fashion?

To start with, when you sit down to a meal, take a moment to register how you feel. Your Child-like attitudes are emotional, not cerebral. Give yourself some space to let those feelings float up to the surface so you can acknowledge them.

Again, using your Learning Journal pages to make notes, decide on several changes and see how that makes you feel. For example, you could practice leaving food on your plate once you reach the point of fullness (not forcing yourself to 'eat it all up'). Avoid hoarding sweet treats, and explore your diet. You don't have to eat the way you always have – you can choose from now on.

Stop and consider why you are moving towards the fridge/cupboard – ask yourself if you really are hungry, and what has just triggered this thought/action?

When one biscuit isn't enough – an end to binge eating
Is this you? Notice what you feel in acknowledging this.

Scientists are particularly interested in the way our brains seem to support comfort- and binge eating instead of preventing it. According to a team led by Kay Tye, Assistant Professor of Neuroscience at Massachusetts Institute of Technology, USA, in research published in the journal *Cell* in January 2015, there are specific neural pathways which transmit feelings of reward when we overeat sugar, developed perhaps to encourage consumption in times of famine when food became transiently available.

Tye says: 'We have not yet adapted to a world where there is an overabundance of sugar, so these circuits that drive us to stuff ourselves with sweets are now serving to create a new health problem.' Does that mean overeating is inevitable? Not at all. The brain's natural plasticity – its ability to re-draw its neural pathways – means we can embed new messages of reward and support through behavioural change.

These old pathways were important to our ancestors, but in our modern times of consistently plentiful food (indeed over-supply), we need to analyse our motivations for eating too much. Ask yourself what is the trigger for the first biscuit? Perhaps you are having coffee with a friend and enjoying some biscuits; there is nothing wrong with that. What we are talking about here is the 'closet-eater' – the one who consumes a packet of biscuits or a family-sized bar of chocolate at a time. If this is you, are you aware of any feeling of secrecy or hoarding around food, whether you live alone or not? How else does it make you feel? Comforted, happy, full, sad, sick, guilty, or full of self-loathing? The fact that you may feel any of these emotions regardless of whether you live in company or alone is a good indicator of why this is a self-boundary that needs work.

If you want to stop binge eating, you need to identify the triggers that inspire this behaviour. It may be certain tasks that take you to the biscuit tin, like dealing with paperwork or relationships. If you think back over the past week, look at a time when you know you have done this and consider what had happened just before. You might be at the biscuits not because you feel hungry, but because you had a row with someone close. So, what might be a different response to the row?

It could be that rather than opening the biscuit tin, you open your heart and compose a 'no-send' letter expressing how you are feeling. 'No-send' is the important part. Once you have written that letter – ideally by hand – stand up, take some breaths, get a drink of water, and re-read it. What action could you take now? Do you need to talk to this person? Do you need to confide in someone else?

Is it a repeating pattern of feelings that are not being expressed out loud that is sending you to the biscuit jar? Beware of swallowing difficult feelings with food. You can't escape from those feelings. When the biscuits have gone, the problem will remain and you will now have increased the discomfort. Ask yourself how often you overeat through sheer happiness? You may have a celebratory glass of fizz or a slice of cake, but happiness rarely seems to drive the need for regular overconsumption.

Being aware of the trigger can help establish that self-boundary (and we look at how to deal with difficult relationships and boundaries with others in a later step).

Mixed messaging

Some people reading the lists at the start of the food section will have agreed with statements from both lists. The dialogue across your internal debating table might look like this:

'Food costs a lot of money, you need to eat what you're given.' (A Parental voice.)

'Yes, I'll eat everything on my plate.' (A Child-like response.)

You need to think about all the messages equally in order to get to an Adult place. So, you could reframe those statements this way:

'The food costs a lot of money but I know what I can afford and I stick to that budget.'

'I use that food to prepare a portion size that is appropriate to my needs.'

These statements come from a healthy Adult place where your eating habits are decided by sensible here-and-now arguments, not historic feelings or orders.

Aspirational eating

Why does food have to be good or bad? Proponents of the new healthy eating – often displayed on an Instagram post and hash-tagged #cleaneating, #purefood and #fitfood – seem to be defending a non-processed food diet. At a time of obesity (where manufactured food is sometimes associated with high salt and sugar content) what's unreasonable about that? Shouldn't we all try to eat more like our ancestors did – wouldn't that end the obesity crisis?

Many dieticians would agree that food with fewer additives can only be better for you. However, the trend towards eating in an aspirational way seems to be more complex and we have a different goal than simply improving nutrition.

There is even a named condition – orthorexia nervosa – to indicate an unhealthy obsession with eating healthy food. Orthorexia was defined in 1997 by Dr Steven Bratman, who intended the name to be a parallel with anorexia nervosa. He says: 'I originally invented the word as a kind of "tease therapy" [a way of using gentle humour to highlight a concern] for my overly diet-obsessed patients. Over time, however, I came to understand that the term identifies a genuine eating disorder.'

Although orthorexia is not an officially medically recognised term, Dr Bratman, a general practitioner based in San Francisco, believes it covers those for whom eating healthily has become 'an extreme, obsessive, psychologically limiting and sometimes physically dangerous disorder, related to but quite distinct from anorexia'.

'Often, orthorexia seems to have elements of obsessive compulsive disorder (OCD), as does anorexia. Some people with orthorexia may in fact additionally have anorexia, either overtly or covertly (using pure food as a socially acceptable way of reducing weight). But orthorexia is usually not very much like typical OCD *or* typical anorexia. It has an aspirational, idealistic, spiritual component which allows it to become deeply rooted in a person's identity. It is most often only a psychological problem in which food concerns become so dominant that other dimensions of life suffer neglect.'

Aspirational eating aficionados have more in common with

followers of other restrictive diets – whether that limit is sugar, animal products, calories, wheat, or whatever. The pleasure seems to lie in the denial not in the physical effect – and is clearly competitive. Witness the hundreds of thousands of posts on Instagram by fans. But medical experts are warning of the long-term health risks of such restricted diets. A recent study, published in *Eating and Weight Disorders* in June 2017 on the connection between social media use and an obsession with eating healthily, concluded that high levels of orthorexia could be found in populations who take an active interest in their health and body and often occurs with anorexia nervosa.

Its results suggest that the healthy eating community on Instagram in particular shares a high level of orthorexia symptoms, with greater Instagram use being linked to increased symptoms. The team led by Dr Carmen Lefevre, a research associate at University College London (UCL), said their results may also have clinical implications for eating disorder development and recovery.

So, ask yourself – do you get more pleasure from posting a photograph of beautifully presented food than you do from eating it? Would you be as interested in eating this way if you didn't get rewarding affirmations from strangers on social media backing your food choices?

It's interesting to note that many progress from one form of limitation (e.g. gluten-free foods despite no specific medical problem with gluten) to another (water-only days) to find the emotional satisfaction they crave. Too little it seems can never be enough.

Neither end of the spectrum brings about a feeling of being OK long term. Denial is coming from that Parental voice in your head; the overindulgence is you at your most Child-like. Neither is you making food choices as an Adult having taken into account all the information available.

Age-appropriate diet

Like it or not, our metabolism slows down as we age and most of us need gradually fewer calories to maintain the same weight or size. Yet it can be very difficult to see that gentle change happening until we wake up one morning and that favourite pair of jeans or work shirt simply won't do up.

You may feel 18 on the inside but if you are 55 in reality, your body will have very different nutritional needs. Part of establishing healthy self-boundaries around your diet means being realistic about portion sizes and types of food.

If you grew up helping on your parents' farm, you may struggle to lose the mindset that you need constant fuelling. Likewise, the 24-year-old junior account executive, who no longer plays sport as she did at school or university, will have to reconsider whether she needs high-carbohydrate meals to fuel her eight-hour shift sitting down. Ask yourself – and make a note in your Learning Journal – am I eating for my present lifestyle or one from my past?

What does an Adult relationship with food feel/sound like for you?

'I don't worry about what I eat; overall, I'm confident my diet is balanced.'

'Sharing meals with friends is a pleasure.'

'I know what is healthy and make sure I eat enough of that.'

'I feel OK with how I look.'

'One biscuit doesn't equal a downfall.'

'I never punish or comfort myself with food.'

'I don't fight or ignore hunger – I take it as something to be attended to.'

'Food is essential fuel, but it can be fun too.'

Having healthy self-boundaries around food means adopting this balanced attitude or approach. Humans need to eat, so denial is just as inappropriate as over-indulgence. Turn to your Learning Journal pages and make a note of what self-boundaries you are going to put in place regarding your eating habits.

Unhealthy Habits

Here, we're going to tackle the not-necessary habits which many people accumulate and find hard to shift – from alcohol, cigarettes and prescription and non-prescription drugs to online porn.

We drink, don't we? Champagne to celebrate, Prosecco to mark the end of the week, a glass of rosé on the first night of summer, G&Ts in the interval at the theatre: somewhere during the 1980s drinking regularly, perhaps at home, and even alone, became acceptable for women and men in a way previously unknown.

Some of us smoke – fewer than in the past, you might think. Yet one in five Britons is still a smoker, according to the Health & Social Care Information Centre.

There are also increasing issues with over-the counter (OTC) drugs containing codeine or non-prescription sleeping tablets. One in three people aged between 18 and 24 now take OTC pills once every 24 hours, according to a report by OnePoll – often at the slightest hint of pain, research reveals. And let's not forget those taking legal highs, illegal drugs such as cocaine or cannabis, or habitually viewing pornography online. They may describe this as recreational behaviour – but what an odd word to use about something that is potentially dangerous.

As with the healthy guidelines around food, you would really need to be living on a remote island with no Wi-Fi to not know that smoking has been linked to numerous serious illnesses, that codeine dependency is a real concern for GPs and what the healthy levels are for alcohol consumption. Indeed, the latest guidelines from the chief medical officer for England recommend abstaining from alcohol for at least two days a week and stress that there is no 'safe' alcohol intake and even drinking small amounts could contribute to diseases such as cancer.

So, the facts are there: on the radio, in magazines, on TV and on the Internet – but even so, are you like the 'three wise monkeys' when it comes to your unhealthy habits? See no evil, hear no evil and speak no evil: just get the bottle open.

We'd encourage you at this point to think about whether you feel in thrall to a habit (be it a tranquiliser or a joint) and no longer in control of this situation.

EXERCISE: The Pasta Jar

What was your reaction to this section? Did you think – 'this is nothing to do with me, I have no bad habits'? Or perhaps, 'people always worry too much about me drinking/smoking, but I am totally in control'? Or maybe you wondered if you rely on your habits too much and are afraid to examine them more closely?

Take a bag of dried pasta and a large clear glass jar or vase. Every time you indulge your habit – have a glass of wine/cigarette/painkiller, for example – you are going to place one pasta piece in the container. But here's the twist, we also want you to place a piece of pasta in the jar every time you *think* about your habit as well.

Be as honest as you can. Every morning when you wake up, take a picture of the jar on your phone so you can compare them at the end of the week. You may be surprised which day saw the most pasta placed in the jar. Think through the day and note down in your Learning Journal what you believe happened that triggered the urge to turn to your habit.

At the end of one week, congratulate yourself on completing the exercise. Now take a look at your jar (or jars). What is your response to the final jar? Are you surprised?

It might be that you have less of a problem than you thought. Is there cause for worry, or does it feel as if you have been 'good'? Have you been completely honest with your pasta jar?

This is the start of you gaining a clearer understanding of what's going on. Don't be self-critical at this point; be kind to yourself. This is about arming yourself with information you can use to help draw a new healthy self-boundary.

BRING IN THE BOUNDARIES:

Your Unhealthy Habit Plan

Picture yourself at your debating table. In the middle of the table is your habit of choice. In this example, we'll refer to a bottle of wine but you know the item that would be there for you. Now, cast your eye around the table. What is the reaction from your different selves to this item? Make a note of this in your Learning Journal and really consider the thoughts and feelings that go with that.

Let's picture a bottle of Sauvignon Blanc on the table. A controlling parental voice might be saying, 'What's the fuss? A drink before and with dinner every night is what we do.' A rebellious child might be saying, 'Yippee! I can have as much as I want.' Another child voice might be saying, 'I don't like the taste but if I have a drink I can be more fun.'

The voice that may be missing is the nurturing parent saying, 'But what's best for us?' Note that the Adult at the table will be weighing up the opinions but perhaps cannot get a word in edgeways for all the chatter going on. Many people will recognise this sense of internal debate which seems to accompany habitual behaviour. You may even feel the urge to reach for a bottle in response to the mental chatter as a way of silencing it.

So, what's going on? Once you commence the habit you are knowingly shutting up the Adult voice, forcing them away from the debating table altogether to prevent their moderating influence on the internal melee. Another way of looking at this is to imagine that the consequence of your 'bad habit' is to allow the Child and Parent voices at your debating table to run the show with all the chaotic results and misunderstandings you can imagine.

This internal debate will have a knock-on effect not just on how much time or energy gets put into the habit, but on your external behaviour too.

For example, the critical parent voice, being judgemental and defensive, may get free reign and you might hear 'you don't know how to behave' or 'you're useless'. These types of remarks are directed at yourself or let loose on others. Alternatively, indulging in our habit may see that internal Child let out to start dancing on the table and ignoring societal conventions, resulting in risky behaviour.

So, who were the loudest influencers around your table?

If it's the child, perhaps you need more opportunities to let go in your life? If that one glass too many equates to the only time you get to dance on the tables, why aren't you letting that side of yourself out in your life as a healthy part of it? Perhaps consider going to a comedy club or taking up salsa.

If the loudest voice is venting spleen at another, what is it you are not saying when you are sober in that relationship? If the anger is voiced at yourself, why are you so harsh on yourself? If you are dealing with this quietly every day, then the lack of self-kindness needs to be addressed.

Remember: a healthy self-boundary means taking all of those voices into consideration, but the Adult makes the decision.

So how about creating some healthy self-boundaries instead, whatever your habit. Bear in mind that habits can travel in packs. Changing one may well inspire a healthy knock-on effect on others, so if this sounds like you, start with a self-boundary around one habit that feels doable. Once that boundary feels secure, you can work on the others. Here are a few tips:

- No 'day off' your habit? Ask yourself why that is. What is keeping you in this habit? Take a 'day off' a week as a starting place; make sure that day has something nice in it, like a special meal, luxury bath, dance class, game of footie, or favourite TV show.
- Once the first day is established, you may notice you are pleased to be in charge – and not the habit. Think about your pasta jar.
- Make it difficult to indulge your habit. Don't keep quantities to hand – whatever it is.

If you notice that you really can't or won't put changes regarding your habits in place, do talk to a professional about it. You might need some extra support to help you make the changes.

Draw the Line: *parents know what's best for their children, but all too often fail to offer the same level of care for themselves.*

See yourself making changes to your unhealthy habits not as a series of denials but as chances to add to your quality of life and experience. Habits mean what they say – you keep doing the same thing for the same reason, but not understanding your motivation and so you don't reap the reward you really need. For example, if you can't sleep without a sleeping pill, wouldn't it be better to establish the cause of your insomnia and treat that instead? Or to resolve the stress that has you reaching for a cigarette or bottle every evening?

Note down how you feel now about your unhealthy habit and what action you intend to take in your Learning Journal.

Social Media and E-mail Protocol

Now we are going to look at your online life, social media and the ubiquitous overflowing inbox which seems to demand attention all the time. It would be difficult to find someone who received hundreds of letters through their door every day – all of which needed opening and reading - yet who doesn't see a deluge of new e-mails every time they log on? We all know that most will be junk of some kind, but that doesn't ease the fear that among the links to supermarkets and notifications of sales, there isn't one crucial message which must not be missed. We're confident that drawing a line around your inbox is one boundary everyone will benefit from – and learn to enjoy too.

We will also show you how to assess the time you spend staring at screens and how to build a healthy boundary around your Wi-Fi use. We also cover using self-boundaries when establishing or seeking friendships online, the shaming phenomenon and online safety.

By the end, you will have a clearer idea of your own relationship with the online world, and the tools to create healthy self-boundaries so you can navigate it more securely.

Draw the Line: *your phone is not human, merely a conduit. Remember that none of these conversations are face-to-face.*

When we say social media, we're including every kind of interaction and relationship online, whether it's someone you know on Twitter, a business contact on LinkedIn, a gamer friend on World of Warcraft, or family members on WhatsApp: the same basic rules apply to all these online communities. After all, social media is not the preserve of teenagers on Instagram. We're all at it – in some way at some time. For the first time, more than half of all online adults who are 65 and older (56 per cent) use Facebook. Roughly half of Internet-using young adults aged from 18 to 29 (53 per cent) use Instagram. And half of all Instagram users (49 per cent) use the site daily. The share of Internet users with college educations using LinkedIn reached 50 per cent. And women dominate Pinterest: 42 per cent of online women now use the platform.

So, how much time do you spend on social media every week? You may be staggered to know that the average adult is probably online almost a full day and night each week. According to the communications watchdog Ofcom, in its *Ofcom's Media Use and Attitudes 2015* report, the average adult spends more than 20 hours online a week (which includes time spent on the Internet at work). And 2.5 of those hours are spent 'online while on the move' – away from home, work, or place of study. Young people aged between 16 and 24 spend more than 27 hours a week on the Internet. It's practically as much time as you spend in a full-time job.

Of course, much of that time will be related to work. And surely, it doesn't matter if we then check in with our friends through Facebook after work … We can spend as long or as little online as feels good, can't we?

Well, perhaps not. The medical community are increasingly

warning of injuries related to overuse of Wi-Fi-related technology, including repetitive strain injury and back problems from too much intense use of phones. A 2014 study found that looking down at a mobile is the equivalent of placing a 27kg weight on one's neck. According to Kenneth Hansraj, a New York back surgeon, writing in the journal *Surgical Technology International*, an average human head weighs about 4–5kg, and tilting it down to check Facebook, send a text, or to Google the weight of a human head increases the gravitational pull on the brain. The stress this places on the spine, Mr Hansraj says, 'may lead to early wear, tear, degeneration and possibly surgeries.'

What is more worrying is the effect of all this online activity on our mental health and relationships with others. A Columbia University study has found that we are becoming so adjusted to using Google that our brains are rewiring themselves so that we look to information online before using physical maps, reference books or, crucially, asking other humans. The research, which was published in the journal *Science* in 2011, says: 'It may be no more than nostalgia at this point, however, to wish we were less dependent on our gadgets. We have become dependent on them to the same degree we are dependent on all the knowledge we gain from our friends and co-workers—and lose if they are out of touch. The experience of losing our Internet connection becomes more and more like losing a friend. We must remain plugged in to know what Google knows.'

But what happens when your usage creeps up so much that it starts to affect other parts of your life: like health, sleep, or relationships? (There is a particularly strong link between a good night's sleep and clear boundaries around Wi-Fi use.) This is when you need to examine all your self-boundaries and perhaps think about ways to strengthen the appropriate ones here.

Online Audit

Let's establish how much time you spend online. For a snapshot of your activity, monitor a weekend's usage of your preferred Internet device. This could be your mobile phone but might also be an iPad or laptop. First, notice how long you go without checking it when you wake up and make a note in your Learning Journal. Now, start logging every time you go online and for how long. You could use an app such as Moment to measure how much time you spend on your device over the course of a day. (Make a note if you are consciously avoiding logging on in order to achieve a 'better' set of statistics later.)

It's useful to put down your feelings around your phone. Does the idea of being separated from your device cause anxiety? Do you feel like you are holding your breath or do you feel relieved? Can you remember the last time you forgot to charge your phone?

At the end of the weekend, count up your hours online and offline. Are you surprised (in either way)? If you spent longer online than you imagined you did, do you think time was wasted which could have been used more productively or pleasantly?

The overriding problem most of us have is simply spending too much time online. But the reason it can be so hard to establish a healthy boundary here is that we are likely not interacting with just one source of media.

We go online through a variety of portals – from social media to games to newsfeeds. And at the other end of the connection we are interacting with a variety of people who may or may not be who they say they are.

So, although you can turn off your computer as one way of gaining control, to achieve real mastery of your online time you need to examine who, what and where you connect with. That means examining what is drawing you in even when you know you need to be doing something else.

EXERCISE: The Wi-Fi House

Take a moment to imagine you are standing on the steps of a large and inviting house. It is brightly painted with gleaming mirrored windows you can't see through. Now, add your own touches: turrets, flagpoles, paint colours, window boxes, etc. Welcome to Wi-Fi House!

In your hand appears the key to the front door. Are you going to open the door and walk in?

You've stepped inside and ahead of you is a beautiful hallway – you might imagine black and white tiles or a wooden floor with an Asian rug on it. Perhaps it is polished concrete with an Ercol chair.

There are multiple doors leading off the hallway. Each one has a name plate on. They say: Facebook, Twitter, e-mail, Instagram, WhatsApp, Snapchat, Safari, BBC News, Music, Games and Pinterest.

Walk down the hallway: you'll notice that different sounds/smells exist behind each door. Perhaps there is the clatter of typewriters and the smell of coffee from behind 'e-mail'; 'Facebook' may be the front for the giggles and guffaws of friends; from behind the 'Twitter' door you can hear whispers and arguments; 'Instagram' is shielding the smell of fresh grass and you see camera flashes under the door.

Which doors are you drawn to? And which doors do you need to enter? For example, you might need to enter the e-mail door as you are waiting for confirmation of an appointment. But as you walk towards the e-mail door, you hear the giggles from behind the Facebook door. You may say to yourself, 'I'll just pop through the Facebook door for a minute,' but once in you find it hard to leave. By the time you extract yourself and head back to e-mail, 30 minutes has passed. Do you head into e-mail now, or check the News instead?

Take a moment to consider. If there was a webcam that filmed the inside of your Wi-Fi House and your behaviour, what would you see? How often are you dashing in and out of the various doors? How much time are you in e-mail, compared to the other, more recreational rooms? If you speeded up the film, would it look like a comedy, with you constantly dashing in and out of rooms with no apparent logic or control? Now, leave the hallway and the house.

Have you noticed there are no bedrooms in the Wi-Fi House. Why do you think that is?

And how would you feel if you lost the key to the Wi-Fi House? (We'll talk about how to master your key below.)

Note down your observations in your Learning Journal.

The Wi-Fi House masquerades as a 'home' because you may feel you are connected to others, but you are actually alone. Of course, there is some value in the connections you make and what you learn, and there is no harm in being entertained – as long as you remember you are in control of your Wi-Fi House, not the other way around.

FOMO

FOMO – or 'fear of missing out' – might be something you associate with teenagers who can't bear to miss a party or a conversation but FOMO is at the root of many problems with online overuse. When you have experienced connectivity on this global scale – joining in hundreds of conversations via social media – it is inevitably quite difficult to extract yourself. It's all just so exciting and new, like a modern child in an old-fashioned sweet shop. Perhaps our evolutionary genes are also coming into play: our ancestors knew how vital it was to collect knowledge as a way of staying safe. Maybe we are instinctively doing the same – on a grander scale.

BRING IN THE BOUNDARIES:

Your Online Plan

Here's how to start managing the e-mails in your inbox, your social media and its allure, staying safe online and, most crucially of all, mastering the key to your Wi-Fi House.

E-mail protocol

We talked in the introduction about Victoria's e-mail exchange, which was hugely improved by the introduction of self-boundaries.

Let's take a moment and reflect back on the body of Victoria's first draft e-mail:

'I am so sorry to say that I feel I cannot help with your plans towards putting on this event. I am really busy with work and childcare at the moment, so am finding it hard to make time. Obviously, I will still do what I can to be useful and don't forget to ask me to invite those people we mentioned, but I think that will have to be my input for now. Do call if I can do anything else.'

After reading it, Jennie says she pictured Victoria and the other person standing on either side of a large lobby in a railway station – in between them are lots of different-shaped bags. When one looks closer at the bags, they all have different labels. These read, variously: 'I am sorry', 'Help me', 'Watch me, I'm juggling', 'Look how busy I am', 'Don't forget, actually I am still helping you' and 'No, really, I will help you'. But there is also one very small packet over on the lost property desk, labelled 'I can't do this'.

Victoria looks confused. The other person standing there looks bewildered, too. She is being invited to pick up a bag, but which one?

So, let's analyse these messages:

Label number one says: 'I am sorry.' In the recipient, it might provoke a compassionate response of 'Oh, poor you' and 'Don't worry, I can do it all.' Or it might provoke a critical response – 'You flake'. It may even prompt a sulk.

Label number two says: 'Help me' – a clear prod to indicate, 'I can't help myself.'

Label number three says: 'Watch me, I'm juggling' – that one demands praise back. It might be met with understanding – 'Yes, you are *so* busy, I don't know how you do it.' Or it might invoke competitive tiredness, 'Well, I'm just as busy and I manage.'

Label number four says: 'Look how busy I am.' This is more blunt: 'Feel sorry for me and also admire me.' Responses will be as before but more extreme. The 'polite' response of convention will probably be 'Yes, you are so busy and we all admire you,' but underneath may be simmering all kinds of resentment.

Label number five says: 'Don't forget, I am still helping you.' This refers to the promise to alert colleagues to the event and perhaps is meant to look generous, but is rather manipulative as it tries to soothe the sender's guilt, reassert their position and attempts to stave off accusations of unhelpfulness.

Label number six: 'No, really, I will help you,' is the most confusing of all. Readers of the e-mail may not know if you are going to help after all.

Don't forget that little packet though labelled 'I can't do this.' This was the whole purpose of the e-mail but it is stuck in lost baggage.

How likely is the reader of the e-mail to see that first, if at all?

Instead they have been left to read between some pretty confusing messages, which Victoria didn't even realise she was sending.

How often do you think this is true of the e-mails you send? Make a note of language you use in e-mails which might be the equivalent of one of those baggage labels. Do you over-promise and then find yourself backtracking, a particularly easy trap to fall into on e-mail or text as you know your facial expressions or tone of voice can't be read?

Draw the Line: *don't forget, all adults struggle with the tone and content of e-mails and electronic communication; none of us learnt this skill at school. We are all newbies together.*

Here are some ideas for applying self-boundaries to improve your e-mail etiquette and control your inbox:

- Pause button. Before you send an e-mail always read it back for extraneous sentences like the ones in the example. Ask yourself whether you really need to provide lengthy explanations or justifications. You might like to add a sticker marked P for 'Pause' to your monitor or inside your laptop to help you get used to the discipline.
- Use your Drafts folder to write and store tricky e-mails to give you a chance to edit before sending.
- Set a regular time for e-mails to be received, say between 30-minute and two-hour intervals. No one needs e-mail instantaneously or constantly, and the beep of an e-mail arriving can distract you from work, and may pressure you into replying hastily.
- Separate work and personal e-mails.

- Never write in an e-mail something you wouldn't say to someone in person or be happy to be shared with the world.
- Have a turn on and turn off point. Do you need to look at e-mails at 6 a.m. or at 10 p.m.? Most of us don't. Instead set yourself a boundary of only checking from 8 a.m. to 8 p.m, for example.
- Don't be afraid to block correspondents who annoy or bother you if you don't need to see their e-mails. They can be redirected to junk without guilt.
- You can also redirect e-mails automatically to a designated folder if you do need to see them but they are the kind which cause your heart to sink when they pop into your general inbox.
- Remember, you don't have to reply to any e-mail.
- Don't allow yourself to get CC-ed into a conversation you don't wish to be part of. Ask to be deleted from the group.

Beware the Freudian e-mail

We've all feared sending an e-mail *about* someone *to* them by mistake, or may even have known someone who has done it. Awareness is the key to not sending e-mails by mistake, however, we'd invite you to consider what's really going on in your head. Why are you discussing a problem with a third party and not directly with the person you have that issue with? What's stopping you addressing and solving it?

Start by using the draft box and try writing the e-mail directly to the person you are worried about. What's the worst that could happen? Is this something you can work on – even if only in small steps?

Texting/messaging technique

The hints here apply to all the super-fast methods of communication, such as WhatsApp, Snapchat and texting of course. These ways of keeping in touch are highly popular because they seem to be suited to our fast-paced age perfectly. They are often inexpensive, all age groups can get involved – and by bringing in emojis to our lives, they are fun.

But the margin for errors and mistakes is similarly sharp: no matter how long a message is, tone and brevity can really affect the way the reader feels. In fact, the shorter and faster the method of messaging, the easier it can be to forget you are in a conversation with another person, opening the possibility for miscommunication and hurt. Many older people may find messages from their children read as surprisingly curt, yet the young texter would probably argue they were simply communicating efficiently.

And although they feel transient, it turns out messages can be stored and shared with surprising ease. Even Snapchat, which offers time-limited messages, is not immune – pictures have been captured in screen-shots and shared.

Properly handled, these fast messages are a good way for families to keep in touch, particularly when young adults are taking the first steps towards independence.

Messaging tips:

- Slow down. Fast-moving messages seem to demand fast replies so it can be easy to respond before you've engaged your decision-making ability. You don't have to respond to any text at all. If you feel particularly strongly about something write it as a draft first and then leave it for an hour.

- Be very strict with your friends list. This applies to all social media platforms. Don't add anyone just because they've approached you, or you'd like to increase your number of followers – remember that friendship is not a numbers game – as that may cause you to receive unwanted pictures or messages.
- Don't feel awkward about defriending or blocking anyone. If you are upset or feel the need to protect yourself from anyone, listen to that voice.
- Beware the large group chat. It's easy to forget who is in a large group and hurt someone's feelings. Be kind.
- Who's your hero? It might be your grandparent or a trusted old friend. It might be former US President Barack Obama. Ask yourself whether you would be happy for them to see a picture you are about to send or read the conversation you are engaging in.
- Don't assume these methods of communication are truly private or transient. Snapchat admits that its own messages, which are designed to disappear once read, have been saved and shared.

CASE HISTORY

Nita is a single mum of two teenage girls and came to Jennie to talk about her marriage breaking down. During their sessions, Nita revealed that her daughters' heavy use of their phones was making her anxious, but she couldn't get a grip on it. She felt they weren't communicating any more.

This is a predicament of our times: young people seem more sophisticated in how they use their technology and anyone over the age of 25 can feel dangerously out of touch and lacking in confidence with how to react. The children sense the parent's lack of confidence and the subsequent change in power dynamic can boost their own self-belief in a way that is not wholly real. The child's apparent superior knowledge can act as a good parent deterrent, but if this feels familiar don't be put off.

Jennie explored Nita's own fears around her daughters' use of phones. Nita had been pleased her daughters had friends and were often chatting to them on the phone and had seen this as a positive during a difficult time (her divorce). She admitted that due to her own personal trauma she had taken her eye off the ball a little when it came to boundaries around using the phones. She had even relied on the phone as an electronic babysitter, offering the children entertainment when she felt too fragile or tired. Now, suddenly things had escalated.

Jennie pointed out that it can be daunting to establish a healthy boundary when a situation like this has already progressed so far. Nita admitted she didn't want any more rows at home and had taken to doing anything she could to maintain the peace.

To Nita's surprise, Jennie asked about her own phone use. When she thought about it, Nita admitted that her own mobile use had crept up. And because she had come to rely on cheery texts from old friends and funny photos on WhatsApp to get her through the past few months, she would have trouble scaling her own use back.

She agreed that looking to her own use was the place to start so she could lead by example. Talking to her daughters could then start without a heavy-handed lecture – 'You've got to stop using your phone so much' – which could easily alienate them and be thrown back at her.

Instead Jennie suggested a family talk could begin with new boundaries being drawn up for mobile use that applied to all members of the home. They could start by shopping for a 'phone box', a container where all the phones would live at night. From that new boundaried place, Nita could then start to talk – without fear of criticism – to her daughters about the worry their mobile phone use had caused.

Nita could also suggest that she and her elder daughter look up how to use popular mobile apps such as Snapchat safely via a good online resource such as saferinternet.org. They could then share that positive information with her younger daughter too.

It's worth noting that as a parent you have a responsibility to keep up to date with new forms of social media and apps in order to protect your child. Just because you are not interested in using these types of communication does not mean you can afford to ignore them. Take the new update to Snapchat called Snap Map, for example, which pinpoints your location on a map for all your Snapchat contacts to see. It is possible to remove yourself from the map by adjusting your settings, but you might wonder how many children would do that willingly or consider the potential consequences of being on it. Campaigners have suggested it would make stalking easy, but more commonly, it could lead to children feeling excluded by their peers when they see others hanging out together.

Sexting

Sending naked images or videos of yourself or others, or sexually explicit messages (also known as trading nudes, dirties, pic for pic) is not new, and for many people is a perfectly comfortable part of their relationship. But the online age brings two issues – the possibility of these images being stolen or shared with unintended people, and the fact that these conversations or picture exchanges live on forever in the Internet somewhere, as some celebrities have found to their cost. Privacy can no longer be guaranteed even for the very wealthy or tech-savvy. According to the Internet Watch

Foundation, up to 88 per cent of self-generated images have been collected and shared on other sites.

Where under-18s are concerned, it's worth knowing the current law too: creating or sharing explicit images of an under-18 is illegal. A young person is breaking the law if they share or download an explicit image or video of themselves or a friend while under 18, even if a minor gives permission for an image to be created. It can result in a police caution and being placed on the Sex Offenders Register – not good for career prospects.

Anyone who shares this type of image or video or thinks their children or children's friends are doing so should consider bolstering boundaries in this area (and reminding themselves of the law).

Your natural boundary line may preclude sexting but you feel under pressure to do it anyway. In the throes of a passionate or new relationship that boundary can weaken (even if you don't want it to). If this sounds like you, be honest and tell your partner:

'You are making me feel uncomfortable.'

'This is something I don't do.'

'You are pressuring me.'

'I feel you want me to feel guilty if I don't give in.'

And of course, as with any text or instant message, you don't actually have to reply at all. Sometimes silence is the most eloquent answer of all.

For those of you who are comfortable with some level of sexting (as well as those for whom it holds no interest), guilt-tripping is never acceptable behaviour. Know your level – this may mean sexy chat but no pictures, say – and never succumb to pressure to go beyond your personal boundaries. 'No' by itself is a perfectly good response.

Social media

The effect of the Internet is seeping into all our lives, often when we least expect it, but particularly in the way we build relationships with strangers who may or may not become our friends/colleagues/lovers.

It was not that long ago, perhaps pre-Millennium, that the first time you met someone was the first time you would know anything about them. You would learn their name, what they did, their family unit, what they looked like, how they sounded, perhaps where they lived, but not much more until a second or third meeting. You might have an instinct about whether you liked this person or not, but it could take weeks or months before you felt more confident of them. Your subsequent relationship would be based around a collation of information obtained over a period of time backed up by feelings and practical experience.

They may have told you they were honest, but if you noticed they fudged their share of a bill you would temper that statement with reality. The most external input you'd get might be a colleague or friend commenting, 'So you've met the boss', or 'Aren't they a funny fish?', or 'Now, they really are clever'. But little other information would intrude on that first contact. How different it is now!

Think of E.T., the lovable space alien. Had the family heard via the Internet that an alien had landed near their California home, and was an unidentifiable body shape with no shared language, they would have barricaded in their children – Elliott, Michael and Gertie – and called the police. Their children might have snuck out with a camera phone to try and get footage of this exotic specimen to share via Instagram. Certainly, an online petition would have been started, calling for its isolation and preservation.

And a blizzard of helicopters would have descended on the town as rolling news stations competed for footage.

Had Gertie ever come close to E.T. she would probably have screamed and run away. Instead, lack of pre-judgement and pre-information meant Elliott and his siblings, and their friends, were able to greet E.T. with wonder rather than fear and, accordingly, forge a relationship.

Of course, we can't turn back the clock to a pre-Internet age, and who would want to? Its many virtues far outweigh the much-discussed negatives. However, it has changed without a doubt the way we make decisions about people. But a little advance knowledge and a little sharing of information can be useful too. So, what's the problem?

Relationships used to be formed in a no man's land, a neutral place, because all parties came (on the whole) with limited infor-mation. Modern relationships are increasingly formed with the addition of pre-knowledge and, more importantly, the potential for pre-judgement. Who was the last person you met without looking up anything about them first?

The danger lies in thinking too much. If we make our relation-ships based around what we already know or have been told, we're cutting out the role of feelings. And feelings are just as important as more conscious cogitations – even though we haven't found a way to channel them online.

How to be safe online

So, how do we use the Internet – this incredible resource – wisely, not just in terms of online security, but in terms of specific relation-ship safety? It comes back to boundaries and your self-boundary with the Internet.

Many people find it difficult to switch 'off'; they complain of feeling 'on' all day. Often, this coincides with the computer/tablet/phone being 'on' all day. As a result, they are accessible to the outside world all the time. They know the answer is to power down the computer but are full of excuses.

How often have you heard yourself say: 'I'm waiting for an e-mail', 'I'll just check once more' or 'someone might need me'? These are all speculative and not real reasons (unless you are a transplant surgeon on call or the chief minister of a large country – and even they need time out too).

The truth is many of us have lost the will or just don't think about how to use the 'off' switch which will help us turn 'off' too. The pace of change has been so fast: one day we didn't get e-mails, then the next day we do all our work that way.

So, is it a question of will? Are we expecting almost too much of ourselves as humans? Given that the Internet as we know it has been ubiquitous for only just over a decade, why do we expect to be able to process and control the effects of its change on our lives so quickly?

Just because we can type faster, pick up programmes, learn intricate coding and develop whole social mores based on what computers can do, why do we insist that our thousands of years of social conditioning and reason be overturned in what is a historical nanosecond? Is it possible that in 500 years' time, academics will study the Information Age with amazement at what we could make happen, and how much we potentially let it change who we really are?

EXERCISE: The Key to Your Wi-Fi House[*]

We all have a front door key, and we'd invite you to recall the key which appeared in your hand on the steps of your Wi-Fi House (pages 71–72). Consider this key as the boundary point for your relationship with the Internet and all it offers, inflicts, demands and tempts us with. Remember, it isn't to turn off your access to the Internet, it is to turn off the Internet's access to *you*.

Now, visualise or draw your key. How big does it need to be for you to remember to use it? Where do you keep it – in a bowl, on a chain, a hook, or in a key cupboard?

Decide upon a time boundary – a start and finish time each day when your Wi-Fi is on and then turned off. Picture yourself turning that key and locking the door: notice your feelings. They might include anxiety, excitement, or a sense of pressure lifting. Make a decision about when you will turn the key again so the door can be opened, and then picture a safe place to leave the key.

Start with night times before planning set times during the day too when your Wi-Fi House will be locked. You could also set Wi-Fi-free periods during the weekend and, if meeting up with family or friends in real life, why not agree in advance to all leaving your respective Wi-Fi houses at the same time so you can be fully present together? We are sure you will get used to being offline, and even begin to enjoy the peace it will provide.

---

[*]   Listen to this visualisation exercise for free on Soundcloud at bit.ly/visualise-your-boundary

Internet 'friends'

What sort of people are you mixing with online? And is the Internet the place you spend most time with 'friends'? Do they mirror your offline friends gained slowly over time and enjoyed at leisure, authentic and valued? Or are they friends acquired quickly, possibly lost just as swiftly, the relationship superficial and without the roots that could sustain it in tough times?

We're not saying that all friends online are not good friends – many people forge strong comforting relationships through online support groups or even Facebook. But give yourself a chance really to think about a social media relationship; there is something about personal information online which can make it all feel credible in a way it wouldn't necessarily in the physical world. Is this because facts look more believable written down in type on a computer screen? Certainly, we are still in the infancy of the online world and remarkably innocent or naïve in many ways.

We all need recognition and later in the book we will be introducing you to the concept of 'strokes' and the importance of being seen and heard by others: a very basic human need. This is why we have all found the Internet so attractive as you can always find someone to notice you somewhere and somehow (even if that is by being provocative – or trolling – on a social media site like Twitter).

If you are lonely, this can make you vulnerable to the wrong sort of attention – whether that is someone pretending to be interested in you for romance or simply phishing for personal information which can be used to steal from you.

By using our Wi-Fi House key more often, we benefit from the grounding effect of being present in the real physical world, and the more time we spend here, the more likely we are to gain real human contact and the fulfilment of genuine relationships.

EXERCISE: The Facebook Cull

We're all guilty of adding in Facebook 'Friends' with whom we'd rather not be in such constant contact – yes? Yet part of us struggles with guilt at the idea of de-friending them. Perhaps it feels unkind, hurtful, or dismissive. Perhaps a part of us also enjoys the idea of having lots of friends – numbers are reassuring.

There is nothing wrong with reassessing our Friends list. Are there some people – a teenage nephew, for example – who you do not always want to share your posts with? Perhaps an acquaintance has now become your boss? Perhaps you have risen to a position of authority which requires a certain amount of discretion? Relationships change over time, there is no reason why your Friends list can't reflect this.

If you'd like to reassess your Facebook Friends boundary, try this exercise. Draw a series of six concentric circles in your Learning Journal. The central circle is you. Label the others: Day/Week/Month/Year/Other.

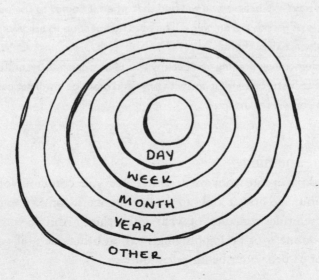

Using your FB Friends list, write the names of your friends in whichever circle feels right depending on how often you would see and talk to them in an ideal world. Now, look at your circles. If we were to suggest you 'culled' the outer circle, how would you feel? Would you feel relieved, threatened, or lighter? Now how would it feel to cull the set of names within the next largest circle?

Having written down these names against how much you are interested in seeing them in the real world, you might feel you want to keep them all. Or you might decide to shed one or more outer circles to reduce the number of people you truly interact with on Facebook.

Now's a good time to get out your debating table. Place on the table the list of names you would consider defriending. Whose voices are loudest around the table saying what you should do? Who is feeling anxious about losing friends? Who is worried about upsetting people? The Adult you at the head of the table asks, 'What do you really need?' Do any of those friendships feed you in any way? We believe you will find that when it comes to the outer circle of friends the answer will be no. The question to ask yourself is why are they there?

Remember, drawing new healthy boundaries can feel uncomfortable at first; stick with it and with time and practice it will get easier and you will feel happier.

Online shaming

How do you rate your own ethics? Are you conscious of your behaviour and how it looks to the outside world, or do you follow your own rules regardless of what others think? And do you comment online – or nod approvingly when others do – if you see someone's behaviour being called out?

Think of a hunter exposed on Twitter for having shot big game in Africa. Would you approve of the hunter being outed, criticised and even shunned? Would you join in (even with a discreet pressing of the Like button or a Retweet), or would you wonder if it was distracting from more serious issues such as the worldwide refugee crises? Do you even care?

We wouldn't suggest there is a right or wrong way to feel about any issue, and if you have a strong reaction to the suggestion of a moral compass, you may be hearing quite loud parental voices (perhaps you were told you 'should' vote Conservative when growing up 'because that is what people like us do').

But setting self-boundaries doesn't mean abandoning all typical codes of behaviour which have developed over centuries. It simply means carefully examining your beliefs so you can choose your own path based around what feels instinctively right, informed by researching issues yourself.

So being told you shouldn't drop litter may well have been a parental order in the first place, but chances are it is one you can agree with as an adult. You may have rationalised that litter does look ugly and may threaten wildlife. Alternatively, you may have been told that eating meat was perfectly acceptable, but you have changed your view as you grew up.

Some people seem to get their views from watching moralising clips online. Perhaps you owe your current attitudes to homelessness and discrimination from viewing this material – or reading the views of popular tweeters, such as actor Emma Watson. Or perhaps you rebel against them, doubting the films' veracity and fighting against being told what to think, especially by celebrities. 'Virtue-signalling' is when someone posts information to burnish their own moral credentials. Think of how public figures bitterly debate the effects and existence of climate change – who is right?

Who owns the ethical position or the moral high ground? And does it matter?

It's worth noting that when you feel the urge to shame someone via social media, you may feel as if you are behaving as a responsible adult, but are you sure? Think back to the debating table. Whose voice is actually the loudest? Is it a disapproving parent, or a child, eager to please and be part of the crowd? What ethical positions have you taken? Were they built from your own research or garnered via the attitudes of others? Have you ever been tempted to join in an online shaming? Think about the following:

- Do check your privacy settings often – at least every month to ensure no updates have altered your basic privacy requirements.
- Never use social media under the influence of alcohol or mood-altering medication.
- Never say on social media something you would be unhappy to verbalise in person face-to-face.
- Do be respectful – not just to those you might want to moan about but also to those who read your postings. Ask yourself, do they really want to read your dirty laundry or second-hand opinions, especially about someone they may well like?

Give yourself space to form your own opinions at leisure, and not in the middle of a heated debate with a group of faceless friends.

Draw the Line: *being an Adult is about taking into account all of yourself. In order to do that you need to consider all your thoughts and feelings.*

When Jennie has talked to clients about establishing self-boundaries around the Internet, and e-mail and social media in particular, she often gets feedback that is not only excited in tone, but also relieved. Quite a lot of us seem to have become so overwhelmed by the demands of an insatiable inbox and too many rooms in our Wi-Fi House that we are allowing them to dominate our lives and forgetting who's the boss.

Note down in your Learning Journal the tips and boundaries you have taken from this section that you can put in place today to achieve control of your online world. Now congratulate yourself on another self-boundary set in place and think about how the extra time and space in your life will benefit you and those around you.

Your Self-Boundaries and Others

Setting these new self-boundaries is going to create or evoke a number of different feelings. We hope it will mostly feel good – but be aware that on the way to developing confident self-boundaries you could feel anxious or fearful. Those feelings may hold you back from completing the task.

Change feels uncomfortable but that doesn't mean it is wrong. That feeling of discomfort when we make a change is positive. And over time, the more you become adept at seeing the need for boundaries and implementing them with confidence, the less that anxiety will accompany your decisions. In other words, it does get easier with time and practice.

Remember, if nothing changes, nothing changes. Use this as a mantra throughout the book.

One particular worry may be the effect your newly empowered decision-making is having on those around you. Considering the feelings and expectations of other people is not an excuse to avoid setting inner boundaries, but be aware of the ripple effect on those around you. Your hard work may encourage others to reassess their own self-boundaries. For example, you may feel other people reacting to your new behaviour, possibly negatively. And like the movement of a boat this can leave a wash which can hit you too, leaving you feeling upset and guilty, and causing you to weaken your new boundary (however much you like it).

Ideally those in your life will read this book as well, so not only will they know what is happening to you but they also may choose to address their own boundaries. Because as Defoe explained – and to paraphrase poet John Donne – no one is an island entire unto themselves.

The idea of self-boundaries may sound as though you will keep your relationships at a distance (holding friends, for example, at arm's length) whereas in fact what we are proposing is a way of maintaining and improving those relationships. Good boundaries help establish and sustain healthy relationships – because they make both partners equal and they level the playing field.

Self-care is about being open to 'receiving' help and support and love when you need it from others. In the UK, it's traditional to use the greeting and standard response: 'How are you?' and 'I'm fine.' These are phrases which we all know to be literally meaningless – as though it is inappropriate to admit to needing support. Think, too, of the British 'stiff upper lip' – all very admirable, but actually, taking care of yourself means knowing when to ask for and when to accept help. There is no reason why strong relationships with clear boundaries cannot happily co-exist, with participants alternating the giving and receiving of support.

If you start to feel hard done by or your emotional supplies are depleted, that is your clue that your relationship is not in balance and that boundaries have gone awry. Also, be aware that sometimes you may be leaning too hard on someone else. You might enjoy it because it is familiar and nostalgic (the emotional equivalent of cuddling up to your mother as a baby). So, do you wait for that other person to set a boundary which pushes you away, or do you establish your own, even though you may feel temporarily less supported as a result of your decision? (And it will be only temporary, because your new self-boundaries will grow and become stronger with time and use.)

Ask yourself what you need from those close to you and why are you leaning so hard or giving so much. Choosing to set your own boundaries – however difficult – is the proper start of self-care. Note that doing this will reduce the risk of rejection, something you might have become used to and normalised.

A good example of someone initially happily ensconced by the boundaries of others is novice nun Maria from *The Sound of Music*. Maria is reluctant to leave the safety of the convent to teach the von Trapp children in the first place. When she finds herself falling for her employer Captain von Trapp, she is unable to establish her own boundaries and so retreats to the physical and metaphysical security of Mother Abbess's rules. However, she learns that she is not welcome in the convent. She must find her own space and set her own boundaries – it is not enough to be blindly obedient in the hope that one can rely on someone else completely.

Mother Abbess says: 'Maria, these walls were not meant to shut out problems. You have to face them. You have to live the life you were born to live.'

This lesson helps Maria to shift from allowing the scared Child part of her to govern her actions. She can return to the von Trapp family knowing her own mind and able to create new relationships from an Adult position.

EXERCISE: Taking the Drama Out of a Crisis

Life is full of drama. Think of your own daily environment and the people you habitually deal with. We're now going to show you how to analyse your own feelings and behaviour to understand yourself better in your relationships.

We are going to give a scenario and we want you to note down how you would most likely react and how you would anticipate others behaving. It is the relationships we are drawn to that tell us most about ourselves.

Imagine there's an unexpected power cut at your business at the busiest time of day. Which of these statements most closely matches your likely reaction?

1. 'Oh my God, somebody do something. I've just lost all my work!'
2. 'I knew this was going to happen. Things like this always happen to me.'
3. 'Don't panic, I've got this. I know where the fuses are.'
4. 'Wait till I find out whose fault this is – they will get a rocket.'
5. 'Wretched power companies – they never care for their customers.'
6. 'I've got a dreadful headache. I need to go home.'
7. 'This is not a problem. Let's go to the pub for a while.'

Now, write down which answers apply best to yourself and those around you. Chances are that everyone will react in one of three ways: as a 'Persecutor', a 'Rescuer', or a 'Victim'. We behave like this to invoke a particular response in others. This is due to our upbringing and how we learned to behave around others, especially in order to get what we feel we need from them (and what we perceive they need from us).

For example, Number 4 is a classic Persecutor's response to a situation. They take control and push blame on to others. Number 5 is also the response of a Persecutor.

Number 3 – 'Don't Panic' – is the response of a Rescuer, someone who likes looking after others. They may be panicking as well on the inside, but they can ignore this by trying to rectify a problem. Number 7 is also a Rescuer's response.

Look at Number 6 – the headache is felt by a Victim. They will look for help, pity, support and be struggling with their own thinking. Numbers 1 and 2 are Victim positions as well.

Looking back at the numbers you have written down, does this pattern of behaviour chime with the people you know and with yourself?

We unknowingly move in and out of the roles of Persecutor, Rescuer and Victim throughout our lives in all our relationships, doing so in the belief that this is how relationships work, that it is normal to interact with someone else like this. And we move between the roles all the time.

Read on to learn more about these roles and how can you use this information to understand your own behaviour as well as identify what others are doing.

> 'A wise woman wishes to be no one's enemy; a wise woman refuses to be anyone's victim.'

> MAYA ANGELOU

The Drama Triangle

The Drama Triangle was created by psychotherapist Stephen Karpman and is a diagram we use in psychotherapy onto which you can map your relationships, as we will now show. Start by drawing a triangle with equal length sides, point down. At the top left corner, write a P for 'Persecutor'. At the top right corner, write an R for 'Rescuer'. And at the bottom point, write a V for 'Victim'. This is the Drama Triangle . . .

Take a coin to represent you in the above scenario and place it on the triangle you have drawn. You are now going to see how easy it is to move between roles.

When we suggested there was a power cut, what was your first feeling? This is where you start. We all have a favoured 'starting position' on the Drama Triangle, but it needs to be stressed at this point that despite the potentially emotive label, no role or place is any better than any other. Nor do you need stressful or extraordinary circumstances to find yourself in any of these positions. We may be on the Drama Triangle any or every hour and day of our lives until we learn how to change.

The first thing we want you to do is to understand your own process – why you take up the position or positions you do. And then to use that information to move away from the Drama Triangle altogether.

Movement on the triangle can be rapid or can be played out over weeks, months, or years. So, the 'Victim' who went home with a headache may have felt rotten for the whole day and the next one, but when they return to work and the impact of this time off hits home, they may become a Persecutor of others, looking to pass blame. They might end up criticising someone who was supportive initially (a Rescuer), who now feels underappreciated – and slips into being a Victim.

Now think back to the statements above – how many can you imagine feeling? As you consider this, move the coin around the triangle to each corner in turn.

You will be getting an idea of how fluid our feelings and behaviour can be, and to understand how we can act in so many ways so fast. This exercise may make it easier to understand those around us, who are going through the same process too.

Let's look further at each position.

The Persecutor (P)

When we are in the Persecutor (P) role, we don't use our capacity to feel but focus on what we are thinking and what we want to achieve to the detriment of the relationships around us. The P's motto is, 'It's my way or no way'.

The hallmark of the Persecutor is that when we are in this role, we lack empathy for the other/others in the relationship.

How to recognise the voice of the Persecutor in yourself:
  You may be thinking:
  'I know what we need to do.'
  'I know what you need to do.'
  'You don't know what you are talking about.'
  'We both know that I'm right.'
  'Do you really think that?'
  'Oh!' (said in a disappointed tone.)
  'Shame!'
  'Why are you crying again?'
  'No one agrees with you.'
  You may be feeling:
  Physically tense
  Hot and bothered
  Cross.

The Rescuer (R)

Again, this character is a strong thinker and what you might call a 'do-er'. Fundamentally, they are different to Persecutors because they have empathy for others. But when we are in Rescuer mode, we lack empathy for ourselves. The Rescuer is all about caring for the other – often from a parental place – best expressed as: 'I know what's best for you really'. This can feel patronising to others, even if it is not meant that way.

Our motives for Rescuing are complex because often we do it to be pleasing and liked. This may be particularly true for those who grew up as elder siblings or young carers, or who were called upon to do lots of jobs for grandparents or parents. They will have become used to receiving recognition for being helpful, but have learnt young not to have expectations of their own needs being met.

How to recognise the voice of the Rescuer in yourself:
You may be thinking:
'I must help.'
'If I don't, I'll be in trouble.'
'You go first.'
'Of course I care.'
'Only I can fix this.'
'You'd be lost without me.'
You may be feeling:
Anxious
Pitying
Excited
Proud.

The Victim (V)

Someone who is in Victim mode comes from a complete 'feeling' place – so their immediate response to any situation is an emotional reaction. When placed in extreme situations, Victims believe they can't think what to do so will look to Rescuers and Persecutors to do the 'thinking' for them. When you are in Victim mode there is a sense of 'bad things always happen to me'. You can feel resentful towards others – everyone else's glass may look half-full.

So, if you are sad because your dog has died and you cry on a friend's shoulder, that doesn't make you a Victim (note the capital letter). But if you then can't leave your friend's house and ask emotionally charged questions such as 'Why does this always happen to me?', then you are in the Victim position because you are looking for more than 'here and now' comfort.

How to recognise the voice of the Victim in yourself:

You may be thinking:

'Help!'

'I can't think.'

'I'm awash with feelings.'

'I don't know what to do.'

'It's all too much.'

'I want to rush out and cry on someone's shoulder.'

'I want to go back to bed and pull the duvet over my head.'

You may be feeling:

Panic

Distress

Helplessness

Smallness

Fragile

Resentful of others

Irritated.

We all have the potential to be somewhere on the Drama Triangle, but we can avoid it altogether. First, we have to understand how we get pulled in. Knowing the role you are drawn to on the Drama Triangle – not just learning to identify the roles others are often in – can help you understand why certain situations arise and the part you play in them. Remember, we have a role to play in any scenario – no one is entirely passive. This is good information because it can help us shape choices.

As we go on through the steps we're going to show you how to alter your own behaviour and avoid these roles through the use of self-boundaries. This is not a manifesto against kindness – we're not saying don't care for others – or don't ask for help. But being aware of these positions and considering where you might be is the first step towards leaving the Drama Triangle altogether.

Conclusion

Now you have worked through Step One, you will have a clearer idea of what boundaries are in general and how to apply them to yourself. At the beginning of the step, we asked you to do a visualisation to picture your boundary. Look back in your Learning Journal to see what you described.

Knowing what you do now about self-boundaries, do you think your original boundary is appropriate? Does it allow you to be in contact with others or is it too rigid and keeps everyone out? Or is your boundary easily breached and allows too many others in? Think again now, what would be your perfect boundary? Make a note or draw this in your Learning Journal. We're going to help you get there.

You can work through the next three sections – work, love, family – in any order you like but we suggest you follow the book as it can be easier to learn to set boundaries with others by starting with acquaintances in the workplace than with lovers and parents, where feelings are more complex.

Step One Summary:

- It is vital to set self-boundaries before tackling boundaries with others.
- Taking care of yourself will give you the tools and the confidence to manage relationships with others.
- Reflect at your debating table whenever you have a dilemma.
- Start with sleep. An essential part of your new self-care is a healthy bedtime routine.
- We all need to find the type of exercise we can sustain in order to maintain a fit body.
- Diet is not a dirty word; educating yourself to eat well pays health dividends.
- If your habits are detracting from your quality of life, taking control will add joy instead.
- No phone or online conversation is as authentic as face-to-face.
- Be the master of the key to your Wi-Fi House; your Internet is under your control.
- Understand and own your role in creating life dramas.

STEP TWO:

THE WORKPLACE

'I put my heart and soul into my work, and lost my mind in the process.'

VINCENT VAN GOGH

We've all heard of the concept of work-life balance, but how many of us practice it? It's too easy to work just a little longer to impress the boss, on the one hand; or to take an extra 20 minutes in the pub at lunchtime when you no longer care to impress anyone – on the other.

Thanks to technology, work has become even more consuming than it ever was. The reality of modern life also interferes with the best-laid plans – as our mobile devices have become ubiquitous, intrusive and often can seem impossible to escape. Would van Gogh have created so many of his 2,000-odd paintings, sketches and drawings had he also been checking his FB page several times each day? It's a sobering thought.

So, establishing boundaries around your work will help you achieve balance on a practical level, improving your relations with colleagues and the boss, supporting you through workplace issues like bullying and romantic entanglements and making work life more pleasant overall. This section of the book applies regardless of whether you are employer, employee, freelancer, consultant, charity worker, stay-at-home mum (it's definitely a full-time job), or intern. We'll still be asking you to complete exercises – remember, there are no right or wrong answers – and keep adding notes to build your Learning Journal.

We talked about social media in Step One, and we've built on that with advice concerning all forms of mobile distraction, engagement and temptation. But we're also interested in exploring those other intangible boundaries that dictate how we relate to our colleagues, bosses and employees, as these relationships are some of the most intense and therefore time-consuming that we have during our lives.

For example, it can be easy to believe that work relationships are crucial to our happiness – how often do you hear people refer to my 'work husband' or 'work wife'? Indeed, a 2006 survey quoted by CNN Money found that 32 per cent of office workers said they have an office 'spouse,' with many having more than one. But that perceived importance is not necessarily based in reality. Their value often lies more in how they affect our outside relationships and the way we treat ourselves.

In the UK, we typically spend 40.8 hours a week at work, compared to a European average of 38.1 hours according to the European Foundation for the Improvement of Living and Working Conditions. If this time is full of tension and conflict on an inter-personal level, let alone tiring and stressful physically, we're setting ourselves up for misery.

Employment Tribes

Learning to understand your colleagues and improve your work relationships is a vital first step towards improving your working life. We've identified five key workplace roles to help you to understand how often boundaries are breached and broken all day every day, and to teach you how to deal with different types of colleagues as well as your own behaviour.

As you read through the characters, note down in your Learning Journal where you recognise yourself or someone you know from your workplace. Be aware – workers may well fit into one or more set of characteristics; indeed you may move from one set to another yourself.

The A-Lister

Always anxious about their health, the 'A-Lister' (where A stands for Ailment) is either off work with 'another virus' regularly, or can be seen seeking sympathy in the office by bringing symptoms into the workplace or constantly discussing them. Not necessarily hypochondriac, the A-Lister's concerns may be quite real.

This behaviour is essentially Child-like and pushes others'

self-boundaries by demanding sympathy, attention and perhaps support with the workload or a difficult boss.

Think of the Drama Triangle – this character is in the Victim position, wanting to be Rescued, but of course also inviting Persecution. Reactions can range from 'Poor you' (Rescuer) to 'Not again' (Persecutor).

BRING IN THE BOUNDARIES:

Your A-Lister Plan

If this is you ...
Ask yourself a few questions:

- Can you remember when you first started to feel constantly unwell – that sense of picking up every bug going around?
- Does this chime with starting your current job or a recent career move?
- Perhaps it coincides with a change in work location or management?

The tangible symptoms of illness (however mild) can actually be a sign that you feel vulnerable and uncomfortable, and the only way to get support is to be ill. This would be particularly true if you are in a workplace you find toxic (either as a Victim being Rescued or Persecuted).

Draw the Line: *workplaces can become toxic. Don't let them poison your thinking.*

Perhaps changing jobs or work locations is not an option, so think what can be done to make working life more pleasant. Can you see where you need to put better boundaries in place? Ask yourself the following questions and note down the answers in your Learning Journal:

- When you are at work, do you take on more than your colleagues? Do you work through your lunch hours? Do you balance work with good self-care?
- Are you in a job you think you *should* be doing, not the one you wanted to do?
- Could you build up your skill set to help facilitate a change when the time is right? Might those skills relate to something you always wanted to do?
- What was your dream job growing up? If your answer is 'I wanted to be a ballerina' – that might seem impossible now, but it's not too late to bring dance and creativity in some way back into your life. For frustrated landscape gardeners, are you missing the opportunity to do something practical, get your hands dirty and connect with nature?

If this is your colleague …

Examine the boundaries of your relationship with them. Think about what you are experiencing.

Do you feel drawn continually to help? Do you stand up for them when other people are complaining, or do you give them the cold shoulder, irritated by their constant whining?

If you've identified that you are a Rescuer (meaning you feel drawn to help them), you will need to redraw the boundary and evaluate your own self-care.

Have you been staying longer to help the other catch up – so they don't get in trouble with the boss? Have you been stuck by the kettle for hours as they offload their symptoms? Notice this will all be having an impact on your own work and life.

Draw the Line: *when we Rescue there is always a cost to ourselves (this may emerge in the short or long term).*

Start with your self-boundary. Only offer help at a level that will not deplete your own resources or affect your own wellbeing. Perhaps it is time to talk to your colleague, to express your feelings and explain your own position and limitations. You may be experiencing this colleague as leaning too far in and beginning to be uncomfortable. Areas that need to be addressed are your need for some space, your own workload which may be building up, your understanding of their distress and your own limits of what you can do about that. It is important to bring yourself back into the picture; this relationship is not one-sided.

So you might say: 'I know you are having a tough time but I am getting anxious about my own workload. I need some headspace to focus on that.'

Perhaps you are finding the current situation so frustrating, you have turned your flexible self-boundary into a solid brick wall. But it's not healthy to be walled in as your bottled-up resentment will become toxic to you.

To establish a better boundary, work to engage more consciously and with empathy both for the colleague and for yourself. Can you think back to a time when work was not smooth sailing for you?

An alternative scenario might be an A-Lister turning to a colleague who moves across the Drama Triangle from Rescuer to

Persecutor. They don't offer hot lemon drinks and comforting words, but are quick to tell the Victim to 'buck up'.

Persecutors need to be aware of how much time they may spend in that relationship with an A-Lister. Even though they may not be voicing their frustration, a lot can be going on in their head, which could then come out at home after work when they offload to their partner. They will be more engaged with their A-Lister colleague than they believe (and possibly contributing to the unhappiness). Being empathetic, but taking a step back, will assist you in moving out of a Persecutor or Rescuer role.

So, what sort of thing could you say to an A-Lister who is driving you mad?

You could ask them: 'What is it you need from me?' This is inviting an open dialogue, rather than allowing yourself to have demands put upon you and instinctively wanting to push back.

The A-Lister may not be able to respond immediately because you are asking them to think, not just feel. If this is the case, ask them to think about the question and what they would like from you, and give them some space to do that. When they come back you can then talk about what you are able to do.

CASE HISTORY

Property solicitor Carmen had been seeing Jennie about her divorce, but one morning spent the whole session complaining bitterly about a 'moaning' colleague, Alex, who was always too ill to do her fair share of the larger, more complex cases their business depended on. Carmen reflected how she had been initially sympathetic towards her colleague, but had become frustrated with the constant absences and lacklustre approach to detail.

Carmen remembered the Drama Triangle and realised that when she was in her marriage, she had fallen into the position of Victim feeling persecuted by her ex-husband. To her surprise, Carmen realised she was now beginning to have Persecutor thoughts about Alex and wanted to address this.

She was able to realise she had initially Rescued Alex – taking on the more difficult, time-consuming cases while dispensing advice and sympathy – but that had then progressed to her feeling angry, resentful and finally moving to full Persecutor mode.

Carmen told Jennie she regretted moving from Rescuer (which felt nicer) to Persecutor (which reminded her of her ex-husband), but Jennie explained that neither position was superior as both reinforce the other person's Victim status.

Carmen chose to deal with her situation by asking Alex what she really needed help with. Her fellow solicitor went away to think about it and came back asking if she could officially reduce her working hours and be given less complex work as she found it too taxing.

This opened up a dialogue about what could be done at work more generally, including Alex finding others in the organisation to give her support. Carmen could then decide for herself how involved she wanted to be.

Draw the Line: *imagine an old-fashioned set of weighing scales. A healthy relationship is balanced. Sometimes one side weighs more than the other but this balances out over time, leaving the balance equal.*

And remember, if you are in a 'dream job' or at the very least enjoy your work, bear in mind that your colleague's behaviour doesn't reflect on you. We don't all work in the same way; their actions are not your concern or responsibility.

The Techno

Technos are our official – or unofficial – IT support workers. And where would we be without them in the modern workplace? However, their perceived superiority and controlling position makes them both irritating and sometimes the subject of fun. Think of the hit TV series *The IT Crowd,* which plays with these stereotypes to hilarious effect.

We may laugh at Technos precisely because we cannot do without them, feeding our sense of inadequacy – especially among older workers, who may buy into the theory that youth always equals more knowledge when it comes to computers. This throws up the intriguing possibility that 50-somethings become more Child-like when computers malfunction or new training is required, and their

20-something colleagues find themselves becoming more Parental in order to balance the equation.

This can leave a Techno frustrated with the slowness of their colleagues' synapses, absorbing their rage and frustration, and not realising that non-Technos can end up feeling patronised and uncomfortable.

BRING IN THE BOUNDARIES:

Your Techno Plan

If this is you ...

So, how do you deal with those around you who you are required to support or lead, but who take out their frustrations on you for faults in the system or their own lack of knowledge?

Ask yourself, what is your job? If your title is something like tech support, then you must approach this differently to someone who has simply acquired the role in addition to their existing job through experience or opportunity.

Perhaps you are officially a Techno but examine your boundaries – have you been trained how to work with others, because operating a computer system and teaching others to use it are different skills? So, if this applies to you, to assist you in establishing your boundaries, you need to request your own support – i.e. being taught how to train others or how to manage, depending on your circumstances.

Also, ask yourself if this type of support or training role is what you want to do with your skills. Would you rather be designing software than supporting its use in an office? What about those who have picked up the techno-support badge unofficially – perhaps because of a natural instinct around computers, or simply a willingness or a pull to help (a Rescuer)?

If this is a position you have slid into, you will need to check your boundaries. Ask yourself how much time you spend on helping others. How are your frustration levels with your own workload?

Conversely, you may have willingly embraced the extra power or responsibility, perhaps because of the feeling of satisfaction at being seen to be clever, or being needed. But this can slip into smugness at your superiority, or may slide into irritation that you are not appreciated enough. You may have willingly embraced a Rescuer position, but others may not see themselves as Victims who need Rescuing. Ask yourself the question, do you inhabit this role in the belief that this is the only way you can be in a relationship with your colleagues? Is this a familiar feeling from way back – that you get recognition through being helpful?

CASE HISTORY

When the marketing firm where Peter worked was issued with new computers he seemed to be the only staff member who really got the new system – even though his job was in the finance department.

Around the water cooler, none of the staff had much common ground with Peter and he was generally considered a bit awkward and not easy to talk to. However, they all happily grew to rely on him if the computers went down and his boss was delighted as it meant she could avoid calling in expensive outside IT support.

Peter was in the Rescuer position – and enjoying it. For the first time in a long time he felt needed and liked as a direct result. He was keen to maintain this newfound status, and particularly the way it made him feel included in company dynamics, especially when he heard people say: 'Where would we be without Peter?'

However, his newfound popularity came crashing down when his expertise was called into question one day. It emerged he'd been seen pulling leads out of the back of a PC, only to 'fix' it later that same day by allegedly just re-plugging them in. The gossips around the water cooler claimed he had faked this issue and questioned the validity of all his previous help. His stock as IT expert – despite previous useful and real contributions in this area – plummeted and staff distanced themselves once again.

Peter had moved from Victim to Rescuer and back to Victim, and was left feeling lonely – a familiar sensation. Who could blame him for asking: 'Why do these events keep happening to me?'

His own questions needed to address his role in the department. Would it suit him better to move into an official technical support role rather than having to create one? Could he volunteer for IT training?

At a deeper level, was this the time for therapeutic support to help him change the pattern of learnt behaviour? If he was able to acknowledge his loneliness, could he find a hobby, club, or learning experience outside work which would improve his confidence and social skills, and give him something interesting to bring into work, to help him build healthier relationships with colleagues?

If this is your colleague ...

How quickly do you shift to behaving like a Victim when it comes to technology and asking for help before even attempting to work things out for yourself? Thereby, being the Victim waiting for someone like Peter to Rescue you. Do you take pleasure in considering IT a 'little bit beneath you' – so people 'further back down the office food chain' can sort that out, while you have more important things to do. This would be someone inhabiting the Persecutor role.

Both of these actions deny you the chance to behave like an Adult – addressing what you can achieve for yourself to aid you getting on with your work, and being appropriately grateful for help if you really need it.

Draw the line: *a healthy self-boundary does not disrespect others.*

The Bully/Bullied

These are such a classic pair of related roles that every workplace probably boasts a couple, if not more. Even if you are outside the direct influence of the dynamic, you may feel its ripples.

If you are the Bully ...

Ask yourself this: do you find a colleague endlessly irritating and do you notice you have a lot of *should* thoughts around them – they *should* be on time, or they *should* do a better job?

Do you believe they are not up to their role, task, or job? Do you denigrate them to others (including at home at the end of the day)? If you know this of yourself, however uncomfortable it may be, take a minute to think what you may be feeling underneath:

- Do you actually feel threatened or insecure in some way (not necessarily related to this staff member)?
- Do you notice the reactions of colleagues you like to your behaviour – and are you comfortable with that? For example, do workmates avoid you or look away when you are interacting with a Victim?

- Do they change the subject when you complain, or do they join in a little gleefully?
- Are you aware of playing favourites – of creating a golden circle or being part of one, perhaps just so someone can get locked out?

If you are the Bullied ...

- Is being treated badly or spoken to unkindly or ignored a familiar experience?
- Can you admit that you feel some attention is better than none, even if it is negative?
- Do you make excuses not to go to HR or your boss to report what is happening or to get the help you need?
- Do you believe there are no options? Do you think this is the normal cut and thrust of any office and therefore acceptable? But do your loved ones worry about your workplace on your behalf?

Day-to-day life in an office can feel like driving on autopilot; we all know what we're doing and interact without necessarily much thought. But when everyone is disengaged like this, offices can become toxic as no one is practising self-care. We'd encourage you to switch off the autopilot for good and be more present when you are at work, however long you have been in the same job and however well you know it.

We're not suggesting you are responsible for everything that happens around you, but you'd be foolish not to be aware of what's going on, so you can moderate your behaviour and take care of yourself as necessary.

CASE HISTORY

Susie landed a job on reception at a local estate agency, having made clear that this wasn't her desired post – which was to be a negotiator – but as a means to get there. While working on reception, she found all her colleagues friendly and reasonably easy-going.

After a year, when no promotion had been offered, Susie reluctantly found a job elsewhere. Her boss finally offered her the role of junior negotiator at 6 p.m. on her last day. Delighted, Susie accepted and was able to share her good news with some of her colleagues that evening (which was meant to be her leaving drinks but turned into a celebration).

On Monday morning she arrived to take up her new position and was expecting all her colleagues to be pleased at her promotion. However, Shirley, a 55-year-old negotiator who had been with the firm as its only female estate agent for years, at first greeted Susie with surprise, thinking she had got the date of her departure wrong, and appeared dumbfounded when Susie explained enthusiastically that she was staying on in her much longed-for new job. From that day on, Shirley stopped talking to Susie and made it clear to everyone in the office how much she disapproved.

Susie felt shocked and tried to win Shirley over to no avail. In fact, it seemed to make Shirley's behaviour worse. Gradually, Susie moved from feeling upset to feeing scared and victimised, and sought help from the boss to no avail. Even the fact she was doing her dream job began to feel like no compensation. Susie began to suffer stomach aches and to dread Monday mornings.

Shirley carried on her bullying via non-verbal cues like eye rolling and murmurs of disapproval at whatever Susie was doing. She made it clear she never wanted to be in close proximity to her younger colleague. The upshot was that due to lack of managerial support, Susie ended up leaving.

So what was troubling Shirley, and what could Susie have done differently, if anything?

Shirley was used to being the special and only female in that position and enjoyed the kudos she felt it brought. She would also play the Victim role, working chaotically and getting the male staff to help her. When Susie was promoted, she felt immediately threatened.

If a pause button could have been pressed at this point, and Shirley been helped to understand what was going on for her, all the unpleasantness could have been avoided. Rather than persecute Susie, Shirley could have chosen to mentor her and won herself new respect, not to mention loyalty, from her younger colleague.

Could Susie have done anything differently herself? Certainly, she attempted to break the ice with Shirley and when that failed, went to her boss to ask him to intervene, which he failed to do. A healthy step would have been to have noted down all the incidents of bullying behaviour in a diary which could be shown to HR and the boss. Even had this not proved useful in the office Susie would have her own evidence, which would confirm these events were real, not her imagination. This is self-care in action: by filling in the diary Susie would have been demonstrating to herself that she took the bullying seriously even if others chose not to.

In the end Susie felt she had no option but to leave, as the office atmosphere was too poisoned.

Sometimes, the hard truth is that you cannot turn around a bullying situation when you are the one being bullied (the Victim), or even if you are an outsider to the Bully/Bullied relationship. You may be better off improving your environment in a different way, which may mean leaving it or toughing it out.

Draw the Line: *the world is not perfect; not every relationship can be saved, nor needs to be.*

BRING IN THE BOUNDARIES:

If You Are Being Bullied Plan

How do you deal with this? Let's go to your inner debating table. There may be lots of noise, but the dominant voices will be from the Child part of the table, being backed up by a critical Parent. So, what you will notice is that there will be little Adult heard.

One Child could be saying, 'I want to run away.' Another could be saying, 'I'll stay close to the bully so I can keep an eye on what is coming and, who knows, maybe if I'm really nice to them, they'll stop.' A Parental voice could say, 'You deserve this treatment. You are not working hard enough, you never do.' These tips will help you listen to your Adult at this time.

- Be aware – like when you learn to drive – of everything that is happening around you. Notice how other people react to the bully. Do they get as upset as you or are they able to shrug off bullying behaviour? Ask yourself if your reaction is proportionate.
- Are your friends in work or outside? Are you spending too much time with a work crowd and not getting access to independent support or fresh ideas?
- Read your company's HR policy and empower yourself with some knowledge. It may be more supportive than you realise. Seek out your Human Resources manager.

- If you feel reluctant to talk to HR, you may be listening to your Parent voice too much; that can often be telling you that you should sort this out yourself – or 'get a grip'.
- Alternatively, if you feel that your HR department would place you in a perilous position – letting the Bully know you have complained but affording you no protection – it is worth getting independent advice from an employment lawyer who can act as your advocate. If your bully then tries to engage you directly, you can politely refuse to discuss your case, directing them to your solicitor. You could say something like 'I believe the time has come for us to get some third-party help with this situation.'

The bystander view

Having read all of the above, what if your colleague is the bully or bullied – where do you stand and what might you consider doing or not doing?

Take your perceived-to-be-great work colleague – the bully – who makes you laugh (even if occasionally you wince or worry you are next). Ask yourself what you are colluding with. Would you be happy to be the butt of his or her jokes? Indeed, do you suspect you might be when you are off work? It can feel safer to stay close to someone like that than have a healthy boundary and take a step back.

But by removing yourself as the audience you can starve the bully of the attention they may be seeking, allowing everyone to get on with their work and improving the atmosphere in the office overall.

As for your bullied colleague, it is not your job to Rescue them. And in fact lending too much of a supportive ear might prevent them from seeking the professional help they need. Far better they talk to HR than colleagues in the pub. Do acknowledge how they are feeling and then ask what they are going to do about it. Don't join in isolating them.

Beware! Don't enjoy the dramatics too much as that not only helps perpetuate them but you run the risk of being drawn in and used by either side.

The Yes Man/Woman

This office character is familiar thanks to their obsequious relationship with the boss, which unbalances other relationships throughout the workplace.

CASE HISTORY

Lara works at a prestigious marketing agency, running one of several small departments which all report to the same domineering boss, Steve. Her colleagues tend to cope with Steve's demands, which are always urgent and often unachievable, by keeping their heads down and quietly backing each other up. But Lara decides that her best chance of pleasing Steve is to be friendly. However, her polite compliments – such as 'that's a great idea' – which are well received initially, seem to lose impact and effect over time.

She feels like she is caught in a zero-sum game with ever-rising stakes, where she is praising Steve constantly – even when she knows nothing about the subject – and gets nothing (not even work feedback) in return.

The situation has gone so far that she doesn't even notice her colleagues' looks of bemusement and outright hilarity when she greets her boss one morning, calling out across the office, 'That's a really lovely suit.' Needless to say, her boss is not thrilled at such a lapdog attitude. He can see the potential for ridicule from the wider community and despises Lara for being sycophantic. Lara, meanwhile, feels increasingly isolated and unhappy, and eventually leaves the company to start again elsewhere.

This is a different scenario to the Bully/Bullied roles above but we are again looking at a Persecutor role (the Boss), who has successfully fostered a culture of 'my way or no way'. Others have dealt with him by quietly getting on with their own business and interacting as little as possible, maintaining healthy boundaries and limiting damage.

But Lara, in her attempts to please Steve, has become stuck in child-like behaviour and is not practising self-care. If she is showing herself no respect, how will she earn it from her boss and colleagues?

If this is you ...

Respecting the boss and their style of management is one thing, allowing yourself to be sucked into agreeing with them in situations where your own instincts and expertise would naturally contradict that is unhealthy. And as Lara found, ultimately, it can come at a high price.

Do you back the boss up or support their position enthusiastically – even when your own instincts are saying it's the wrong direction? Do you feel a little hyper around the boss? Are you pleased when she/he compliments you? Do you feel more special than your colleagues – would others call you a favourite or even teacher's pet? Make a note of your thoughts in your Learning Journal.

BRING IN THE BOUNDARIES:

Your Yes Man Plan

Lara pulled the nuclear option by leaving but you don't have to. What would be helpful would be to move from this Child-like position and take an Adult, considered approach.

Think back to your debating table. What would the other parts of yourself want you to do? Can you listen to all the voices and then draw a conclusion?

Here are some practical ways to change your behaviour:

- Start by being assertive with yourself. This will require you to acknowledge the fact that the situation in the office is not working for you.
- Focus on your own work; remember why you were employed and what you are good at. When you feel drawn to look up and give a compliment, stop yourself. This is not about 'battening down the hatches', but staying professional and being open to any communications that relate to your work.
- In doing this, note you are taking steps to care for yourself and build up your own self-respect and protect your vulnerability. Notice that others may register this behaviour and reward it with renewed friendship and respect.

Draw the Line: *choose your friends from among your colleagues with care.*

A final point of observation: what will happen to your relationship with that domineering boss? Possibly they won't even notice you are no longer saying *yes* to all their demands. Certainly, the demands will continue. By taking a more Adult attitude, you don't cure a difficult boss, but you can put an end to your own unhealthy relationship, which may make the working day easier and will improve your self-esteem.

Some bosses will always seek out or create Yes people around them – particularly if they are Persecutor bosses ('it's my way or no way') or professionally insecure. But while becoming a foil to these bosses may seem like a smart survival tactic, it's not a sustainable or healthy way to be. Think – where was the boundary? It was behind you all the time. Not so far back that it turned you into a sulky, defensive child, saying, 'I won't acknowledge this person at all', just a step back into safety and away from too much engagement.

Who's the Boss?

The key to a satisfactory, indeed often pleasant, work life can lie in your relationship with your superiors. In this section we'll look at ways you can use boundaries to strengthen and build these in an intelligent and healthy way: the dos and don'ts of the 'good' employee *and* the 'good' boss.

One basic truth to bear in mind is that an employee–employer relationship can easily slip into some sort of Child–Parent situation if clear boundaries aren't drawn. Many modern offices put in place all kinds of processes designed to help this; you may be used to the idea of line managers, weekly, monthly or annual performance reviews, team feedback sessions and more. All of these are intended to help you find your place within the corporate structure. However, be aware – unless you are confident with your own boundaries, these types of 'helpful' sessions can still see workers behaving in a Child-like or Parental fashion.

Dos and don'ts: good employees

- Do: find out exactly what is wanted of you. If you are not given a written job description, ask for a meeting with your boss, query what will be required and take notes.
- Do: take your job description to a trusted friend and/or colleague for them to read. Ask what they think the job entails. It's easy for us to misinterpret something, especially when we are excited or fearful.
- Do: an honest self-appraisal before you start. You may know where your skills are strongest — and perhaps why you were hired — but where might you struggle or need to up your game? You could revisit this in six months' time, long before an employer assesses you.
- Do: know it's OK to ask questions.
- Don't: think you have to make friends on the first day, or even in the first week. Take it slowly.
- Do: make eye contact, say hello to everyone, but ...
- Don't: launch into your life story. Hold something back.
- Don't: moan if you don't get a pay rise. If you plan on a long career at your present company, sometimes investing in your future means patience.
- Do: be realistic. If you put in extra work, are patient and then ask for a rise at an appropriate time and get turned down, you may have to accept that you have gone as far as you will go in that organisation. It's probably time to look around without rancour.
- Do: respect a younger boss. Unless you drop dead in the office, one day you will not be the most senior member of staff just because you are the oldest.
- Don't: resent this. Stay true to yourself and how you work, but understand everyone gets a turn to be boss.

- Do: know that being promoted might not suit you. Sometimes those who are skilled in the delivering part of a job get elevated into management and hate it. Working to our strengths equals a happier life.

Dos and don'ts: good bosses

- Do: respect your elder employees – because you will be one of them, one day.
- Don't: forget the ones who mentored you on the way up and still need to make a good living even though they may not be on the fast track any more.
- Do: put a boundary around work time. Respect the hours of the contract. If you choose to work all hours, don't inflict that as a necessity on juniors, many of whom will not be paid as much as you, or be as driven. Lead to create a healthy working environment for all.
- Do: consider why you are working such long hours.
- Don't: fear unpopularity. Good bosses can deliver criticism in a fair and non-emotional way. It's not about your employees being friends.
- Do: work on your own skills. Maybe enlist a mentor or a peer (outside your workplace) for a mutually supportive relationship, where you can share worries and compare successful behaviours. Perhaps find a business coach. Being the boss doesn't mean doing it all on your own.
- Do: embrace humility. It's OK to say that a strategy has not worked and that you want to try something different.
- Don't: get personal. That means not dating your staff, not commiserating over drinks, not going shopping for shoes together, or gossiping. You need to keep your boundary in place at all

times. Keep the socialising for friends away from work. It's awkward and confusing for staff any other way.

• Do: remember that this is your protection too from being guilt-tripped by staff who have got too close.

Draw the Line: *fixing and keeping a boundary as far as the job itself allows is the only way to behave like an Adult.*

EXERCISE: The Workplace Drama Triangle

In your Learning Journal, draw a Drama Triangle, marking each point either R, P, or V as before. Now add the names of your workplace colleagues or, if you work alone, those who you interact with (e.g. your suppliers, accountant, clients), placing them on the point of the Triangle that seems most appropriate. A classic office situation might see an overbearing boss as Persecutor, the junior account manager as Victim and you caught in the middle as Rescuer. But don't assume hierarchy defines these roles. A hospital ward might see a Persecutor nurse who finds fault constantly with a senior ward manager (Victim), with a junior doctor (Rescuer) constantly trying to make the peace.

Are you surprised by any of their positions? Do they stay in one spot or move around the triangle? Now, consider yourself: where do you start on the Triangle and where do you move to? Is there a particular colleague you spend a lot of time on this Triangle with? Reflecting on your boundaries, how do they change when you are with certain colleagues? What do you need to do to keep your boundaries in a healthier condition?

Reflect on what you have learnt so far to help you do this.

We're going to come back to the Drama Triangle at the end of this Step, when we'll show you another way to change how you see and behave in relationships on the Triangle.

The Workplace Culture

In this section, we will help you understand how your workplace culture affects your life, challenges your boundaries and how to draw the line.

Does your place of work resemble Google HQ – with its 24/7 worker support, including gourmet meals three times a day for its employees, exercise space and showers and an incredible package of spousal support in the event of an employee's death? Or perhaps it has more in common with the fictional *Mad Men* office, where colleagues of all statuses drank and partied together? Either way, you'll probably be aware that every organisation seems to develop its own culture and character, which you may be required to assimilate into, to some degree.

For some of us the idea of an instant gang is appealing – especially in your twenties, when work is everything. You may have only just left home or put university behind you and are perhaps in search of a new 'family' – and possibly even where you will meet a partner with similar goals. But for many it's a new minefield – full of social and practical hazards to negotiate, not unlike the playground, but where the stakes – i.e. your livelihood and future – may be much higher.

Moreover, as we age the need to have a boundaried relationship with our work becomes more critical as relationships outside work become more important, not least that one with our self.

Draw the Line: *surviving the workplace culture needs very strong self-boundaries, as well as an awareness of the boundaries we hold with others.*

You may be thinking, but what's the problem? Surely a strong culture is at worst merely something which we can clock in and out of, and at best great fun? But if you think about it in terms of how it can affect the rest of your life as well as your professional potential, you may understand more clearly why it's important to spot the pitfalls and make the most of the opportunities.

CASE HISTORY

Let's look at two case histories which exemplify these problems:

Judith is 53 and has worked at a major law firm almost since she left university and is a director. Her husband gave up work 10 years ago to bring up the four children when it became obvious her salary and package of benefits far exceeded his own. After sensible considered discussions, the family relocated to the countryside, he took over the household management and Judith began a four-day/three-night routine in London.

Even though Judith is fulfilled at work and her benefit package improves almost every year, she is aware that the couple are not as close as they once were and that the children do not turn to her first with real problems at weekends, preferring Dad and his routine.

If you were to ask Judith though if there was anything wrong with her working life, she would say no. Any tension she does suffer she ascribes to her increasingly strained marriage. And – she admits to herself at night – her sadness that she seems to be missing seeing the children grow up.

So, what's going wrong here?

Judith can congratulate herself on her trailblazing career, as she exemplifies a new breed of successful working woman, but she may not realise she is also in the vanguard of another type of female first: the businesswoman who may regret not seeing enough of her children when they are young.

We are used to hearing older men make this complaint but for women of a similar age and status, this idea is taboo. However, we are going to start seeing more older women owning up to this regret soon. (We are yet to fully acknowledge the rise of the female workaholic and thus the increase in men who are taking up the household management role is proving to be a new presentation in therapy.)

What is sad is that in the majority of cases the workaholic of whatever gender can't understand the impact that their choice of work practice is having on their family. Of course, some individual workers will behave like this whatever the environment that surrounds them. However, often it is the company culture that triggers or enables the overwork in the first place. And when accompanied by what you could call golden handcuffs – i.e. superb financial recompense – the workaholic is rewarded for their own lack of self-boundaries.

Judith may tell herself that she has to work in this way for several reasons – these might include feeling independent and a credit to her gender, or that she is securing the family home and future in financial terms – but she probably doesn't admit that she is completed in some way by overworking.

Meanwhile the office culture rewards these feelings by associating long hours with promotions and pay rises. And making life less practically difficult by offering on-site yoga classes and a dry-cleaning service. And it reinforces the ties by insisting on the constant use of mobile technology. The iron hand in the velvet glove.

It's clear that for Judith the excitement of succeeding is lessening even though she can't stop working; the law of diminishing self-care returns.

> 'I look forward to the day when half our homes are run by men and half our companies and institutions are run by women. When that happens, it won't just mean happier women and families; it will mean more successful businesses and better lives for us all.'
>
> SHERYL SANDBERG

Meanwhile, Vijay is 26 and works in the City branch of an accountancy behemoth. He believes he is employed with a 'good crowd', who work hard and play hard together. He enjoys a pint at lunchtime – sometimes two on a Friday – and, like his friends in the office, rather laughs at the one or two who go to the canteen instead of the pub.

After work, everyone – including middle managers – goes for a drink to unwind before going home and some nights these turn into what Vijay would call a 'session'. He also plays five-a-side with the office team on a Sunday, sometimes going for a boozy lunch afterwards.

Vijay would deny any kind of drink problem – and he feels quite healthy. He rarely takes any recreational drugs – although if the session on a Friday ends up in a local club, well, what's a line of coke?

He'd like a steady partner but doesn't seem to meet anyone not working in the office – and most of those have either turned him down, or have been happy with a one-off encounter. He has an occasional pang that he is missing something and he's not sure the managers he drinks with really see him as promotion material, especially as he does come into the office with more than the occasional hangover. But he doesn't want to lose his place in his friendship group either.

So how can he get off the hedonistic treadmill which is beginning to feel a little relentless? Vijay's situation is a bit like a love affair – he doesn't feel the need to seek input from anywhere else, he is full. And if one asked him if he had a good work–life balance, his reply would probably be 'yes'. But all of his life is in work, or dictated by its demands. If he lost his job tomorrow, what would he have? Moreover, what would he feel? Bereft, unsupported, sad – losing his job wouldn't just be a practical affair but one which would have an impact on his emotional life too. Would there be an empty landscape with tumbleweed rolling by?

So, in fact, Vijay has an unhealthy work–life balance, triggered by a self-perpetuating culture within the workplace which he didn't set up and probably didn't envisage.

To sum up, it is clearly unhealthy to get all your needs met in one place – and this is true most obviously for Vijay, but also for Judith to a degree. She may feel her husband and children give her emotional traction, but in reality, it is her job that is giving her the unconditional contentment – knowing it won't nag her at weekends or in her words, 'make her feel guilty'.

This is a classic vicious circle – both Vijay and Judith have emotional needs which are not being met (no real love life, missing the children) but taking comfort in the office is easier than confronting reality at home and working on the problem. Yet the more they stay at work, and distance themselves from their true unmet needs, the greater those needs grow.

Have you ever felt joyful to get to the office and considered yourself lucky? Is this your guilty secret? Take a moment to think why work has felt good before you have even started it. Is it money, friendship, identity, social status or escape? Make a note in your Learning Journal.

Think back to Google, where the food is gourmet and the company prides itself on its employees never being further than 150 feet away from a food source. When asked about favourite perks, one former Googler said, 'I thought the benefit I'd miss would be the food, but when I lost 15 pounds after quitting without doing anything, I realised how badly I had been overeating.'

Think of Facebook and Apple HQ, where in 2014, suggestions began emerging that the companies would even pay for young female employees to freeze their eggs so they could delay motherhood to a later and more corporately appropriate age.

'This is a nice perk but of course it's a very personal decision for every working woman,' Kellye Sheehan, of the Washington-based Women in Technology organisation told *USA Today*. 'When to time college, grad school, babies, starting a career, accelerating a career – all of these have huge ramifications in your life and that of your significant other. Is the employer trying to tell us something?

'Agreed, working mothers have a lot to juggle. But you can't let your employer force you into something that doesn't fit your values or personal choices.'

BRING IN THE BOUNDARIES:

Your Workplace Culture Plan

We often hear the phrase, 'Take a long hard look at …' Well, now is the time to do it. The first boundary you need to make is with yourself. Look at the following areas of your life:

- Ask your family for some feedback; you may be used to a constant background buzz of 'When are you going to be home? Do you have to have your phone on all the time?' How about asking them how they really experience you, how much of *you* do they feel is with them on a day-to-day basis?
- If you have children, how old are they going to be in five years' time? Will they still want to play? What would it take to put the phone down and go and play hide and seek with them?
- Think about friends – no, not work colleagues, friends. Do you have someone you have lost touch with and when you stop and consider this, you realise how much you miss them?
- What would your landscape look like if your job vanished tomorrow; remember the tumbleweed?
- Start to take small steps. Make a contract with yourself to; phone that friend, leave work on time one day a week (for starters), get a life outside work and, if you rely on the work gym, join another that you have to leave work to reach. Use your Learning Journal to find small ways to balance your work life with your time outside the office.

Office Romances

Most of us will witness or experience the workplace romance. Indeed, one in five of us will meet a partner during our working lives, according to research in March 2015 by website MiC, and there is nothing wrong with that. Nor is there much to complain of when you are enjoying being a protagonist in a harmless crush. It can be ego-boosting and immensely cheering.

However, not all relationships are among equals and not all are sincere. And any love affair – however genuine – can have an impact on the entire office dynamic, even when things are going well. So, how do you ensure your love life doesn't become everyone else's business? It's back to boundaries . . .

Loving Your Colleagues

First, are you in a relationship already? As we all know, that doesn't necessarily mean you won't be attracted to another – or find yourself the object of interest. If you are happy in your established relationship and have healthy boundaries around your work-life balance, then there will be nothing to worry about. But what if you are already spending unhealthy amounts of time at work and life at home seems to get more disappointing? Perhaps you and your partner have drifted into a companionable rut.

In this case, bonding with someone else over a late-night deadline, or shared excitement when a deal comes off, can be a danger zone. It's easy to mistake the adrenalin surge from a shared professional success or the intimacy of repeated in-jokes for something a little warmer.

Do you find you have holiday owing because you would rather be at work than anywhere else? Do you also avoid talking about anyone in particular to your partner for reasons you can't quite – or don't want to – explain?

When you're on the dating scene openly, your antennae can get quite well attuned to whether a potential partner is serious or light-hearted. But in the office – especially if you don't feel you are 'on the lookout' – it's easy to misread signals and intent. The stakes are inevitably higher, too, as a failed relationship could cost you more than just embarrassment.

You may feel your boundaries are perfectly in order, but beware the workplace lothario pushing on your limits to test them. Maybe they need shoring up?

CASE HISTORY

Jennie's client Clare works at a law firm, where she was teamed with another solicitor, Clive. Clare is married – albeit unhappily – and she took comfort in the office, where she felt respected and admired unlike in her own home. Moreover, she had recently discovered her husband had had an affair, so she was not feeling confident. However, she gradually grew closer to Clive, who seemed happy to flirt with her. This was noticed by the others at work and rather approved of, as he was single and her colleagues knew her to be unhappy. However, once Clare and her husband split for good, Clive withdrew from the flirtatious relationship and actively avoided Clare as though worried she would now want to take their friendship to a more serious level.

Clare was confused and came to see Jennie. She acknowledged she felt hurt and perhaps disappointed at Clive's behaviour. She was also baffled at the reaction from the rest of the team, who seemed unable to accept their favourite 'couple' didn't now get together properly. She could feel the dynamics of the group changing, which she blamed herself for.

She told Jennie it was hard to tell who was most embarrassed out of the group and regular weekly after-work drinking sessions tailed off quite quickly. Clare was relieved when she was offered another job and soon left. Could any of this have been avoided?

Let's take Clare's position first. Clearly, she was vulnerable emotionally but not in the sense of looking for a lover. She was burying herself in work to avoid the pain of watching her marriage disintegrate without realising that overwork was in itself going to have an impact on her life, as the self-boundary which could have prevented that had come unstuck. It is worth noting she did not behave badly or inappropriately, so she had no reason to feel embarrassed. Yet still she did feel left with a red face. How could she have taken better care of herself?

Because of the situation at home excess time was spent at work to avoid the unpleasantness of her marriage break up. What was missing was time away from both home and work – both were all-absorbing. If Clare had had a reliable friend she could have talked these issues through with, possibly it would have helped her feel supported as her marriage came to an end and she would have had less need of support at work.

When we are in a crisis it is easy for our worlds to shrink and it can become harder to reach out. That one outlet could have been the valve of the pressure cooker, keeping her work friendship more appropriately boundaried. From Clare's situation we can learn the importance of noticing when our world is shrinking and not allowing our workplace to become our sole source of 'strokes' (see page 299) and, most of all, not getting all our needs met at work.

It's worth considering what may have been happening with Clive as well. He could be perceived as a classic office cad, latching on to a clearly emotionally vulnerable young woman. But, more likely, he was drawn to Clare's vulnerability, enjoyed being needed, but felt safe from commitment as long as she was married. When reality stepped in and a relationship became possible, he would have been forced to confront the truth (at least to himself) and step back – albeit rather sharply. However, his actions made everyone else feel uncomfortable and saw him labelled as an irresponsible ladies' man. Which couldn't have been further from the truth.

Lastly, let's consider the group's position. It's easy to understand their mutual excitement at seeing a budding romance in their number and the consequent disappointment when it didn't work out. No wonder they felt embarrassed and in turn passed that sense of shame around.

The group has suffered from the ripple effect which goes back and forth – depending on what was happening between Clare and Clive. (The perpetual motion ripple effect is the common factor in almost all office romances as the swell of emotion gets picked up, shared around and washed back on to the original participants.) The group cannot be blamed for this sort of mass feeling – it is up to the individuals to keep their own boundaries firm and in place. Clare's boundary, as we have seen, concerns her attitude to work. But boundaries such as Clive's are to do with friendships, which we will be addressing in more detail later.

EXERCISE: The Cost of Working

We're going to add up the cost of your workplace culture here.

Time: add up the following hours per week: hours you spend working in the office; hours you spend socialising with colleagues; hours spent thinking about or preparing for work; hours spent awake in bed, worrying about any aspect of work; plus hours spent talking to your partner about work. Be honest with yourself: is it more or less than you expected?

Friends: how many friends in real life (not Facebook friends) do you have? I.e. the sort you might go for a meal with, or see at weekends. How often do you see them? Who do you feel closer to: outside friends or work colleagues? When was the last time you organised or created the opportunity to see one of these outside friends?

Reasons to stay on-site: count up how many ways your office streamlines your life by offering perks that somehow mean you avoid leaving during the day. These might include an on-site gym, canteen, physio, GP, complementary therapies and massage, dry cleaner pick-up, book and card shop.

Tasks: have you asked a junior to do something for you that was non-work related? E.g. buy a present, fetch food, or run an errand like getting a prescription picked up.

Take a good look at your responses. Remember the weigh scales – work (including social events) is one side, what is on the other?

Like all exercises in this book, there are no right or wrong answers but all your notes form part of your Learning Journal.

The Family CEO

If you don't work outside the home, but instead are responsible for it and the whole family, how do you describe yourself to others?

Are you a stay-at-home-mum, a domestic engineer, a house-husband, housewife superstar, her-indoors or him-indoors – or do you even get a title? When asked, do you tell people, 'Actually, I don't work. I'm at home with the kids.' Well, in this Step, we'd like to offer you recognition.

From now on, if you are the person or parent responsible at home, start calling yourself the family chief executive officer (FCEO). Without doubt, you will deserve this job title, as your role will encompass so many different areas of responsibility and control, from finance (household budget) to marketing (how your family presents to the outside world) and HR (how your family deals with internal crises) to communications (how you encourage healthy dialogue – both internally and with outsiders).

How do you feel about your promotion? Does it feel deserved? Do you think the rest of your family would laugh at the idea or support it? Note your response in your Learning Journal.

So, where do boundaries play a part in defining the FCEO? Let's use our debating table to explore why we do what we do. Perhaps there is a Parental critical voice: 'This is not a proper job worthy of respect,' or, 'This is a job you are not capable of doing anyway.' Another voice is Parental in tone but supportive: 'I know it is best for my children if I am at home.' But there are Child-like voices too, which say, 'This is fun, we can play all day.' And another one says, 'This is too much like hard work, I resent it.'

Your role models growing up will also influence the views at the debating table. So if you were brought up by a contented FCEO, you may accept your position comfortably or you may feel there is a benchmark which you can never attain.

So what can your Adult self draw from this internal conversation? Where do you notice the loudest voices coming from? What part of you are you ignoring? And how are you going to redress this?

EXERCISE: Who's Who on the Family Board

Answer these questions to help understand the dynamics at your boardroom table:

Who was your FCEO – your father, mother, grandparent, or other – and do you feel they did a good job?

Do you feel you want to live up to that parent – and indeed, do you feel you can?

Conversely, was your role model so lacking you put everything you have into making your children's experience of family different (you may use the word 'better') from your own?

Do you look forward to every day or are you relieved when they are over?

Do you assume that others in your wider family see you in a certain way – the put-upon house husband, the clichéd lady of leisure?

You may have identified that your Parental self is most dominant in how you feel or perhaps it is a strong Child-like voice which is loudest, but how can you get into the pole position which will help you to accept your role as FCEO as both valuable and deserved? Note down your responses to the above questions in your Learning Journal and then read on to Bring in the Boundaries.

BRING IN THE BOUNDARIES:

Your FCEO Plan

First, note down your typical working day – what time does it start and what time does it end? Do you ever feel you clock on and clock off? If so, what is your equivalent of a commute (that transitional period between work responsibilities and relaxation)? Do you take a bath, exercise, chat to your partner, or meet a friend without children – or do you stay on duty all the time?

Do you take breaks – e.g. a quiet coffee sitting down, lunch that is more than left-overs eaten with one hand, or even five minutes stretching? Do you feel guilty if you read the papers or stop to listen to an item on the radio? When you are on holiday, is your daily routine almost identical to the work week?

Now, add up how much it would cost to bring in outside help to do your job – from a cleaner to a bookkeeper, dog walker, virtual PA, taxi, cook, gardener, ironing service, nanny, child's entertainer, sports coach, or life coach for your partner. Add this up to help you see your true monetary worth.

And we do mean work it out: start a list at the back of the book and keep adding to it for every task you do. As a rule of thumb charge £10 per hour per task. We guarantee you will be stunned.

What is almost certain is that you will have a poor time boundary. But consider, you wouldn't do a job that required 24/7 work unless it was incredibly well respected and remunerated (think

Prime Minster/astronaut) yet you accept that timetable at home. Is the work truly never-ending or are you unwilling to timetable efficiently? Or perhaps you need to show others how busy you are? If you value your own role you won't need to do that.

With all this information to hand, let those you live with know what you are doing as anyone would with a promotion outside the home. Why not sign off texts as FCEO or label the family filing cabinet as FCEO?

CASE HISTORY

Monica and her wife Sarah decided that Monica should stay at home as FCEO to care for their toddler twins, with Sarah working outside the home in a traditional, breadwinner role.

During the day, Monica works hard to keep the home clean and running efficiently, with plenty of play time for the children, which makes her happy. But Monica has a nagging concern that Sarah brings in all the income now and she worries that she is not making the same contribution to the family – even though she has never voiced this.

Monica has developed a habit of saving the ironing until evening once the children are in bed and after she and Sarah have eaten their meal. She knows this slightly irritates Sarah as she is constantly asking her to sit down and talk, or just sit and be. But she justifies it by telling her that it is Sarah's work clothes, which cannot be left. Moreover, Monica enjoys the slight feeling of martyrdom it evokes as she knows it reminds Sarah that she is genuinely busy during the day and not sitting with her feet up, watching soaps.

Sarah of course doesn't think this of Monica at all. She works hard and longs to come home for some company with her wife – and some fun. Yet now Monica only seems to laugh spontaneously with the children and Sarah is becoming jealous.

How can they resolve this frustration before it grows?

The responsibility for this one lies with Monica. She is turning her internal self-doubt about her worth in this role and projecting her fears on to Sarah. Reassurance from Sarah would be all very well (and nice) but Monica needs to find her sense of self-worth from within. To do this, she needs to set self-boundaries.

Some of these are practical. So, if the partner works Monday to Friday (as Sarah does), she needs to set her working week Monday to Friday. Then decide what hours she is going to work – 7 a.m. to 11 p.m. is simply not reasonable (nor would it be in any job).

The start time can be set at 8 a.m. – which may be breakfast time. Cuddling a sleepy child is not part of the working day, but mealtime followed by dressing, play groups or whatever certainly is. So if, like Monica, you are awake early, you needn't be tempted to start work early. Sarah certainly wouldn't get to the office if she woke at 5 a.m.

Monica can allow herself to rest in bed or read a book, or if desired, exercise on her own. The working day hasn't started. Monica may feel that breaks are hard to schedule – and that she has to keep going – but what if she redefined the idea of a coffee break to include some fun activity that doesn't feel like a chore? Perhaps it's a 15-minute walk to the swings and back, or sitting down with a coffee while the children do something quiet. To be a good FCEO does not mean entertaining the children every minute of the day, nor does it mean constant multi-tasking.

Lunch can be scheduled the same way – the key is to respect your timetable and be consistent. It's often said children need consistency but in fact we all do.

By the evening, Monica has to remember that not everything needs to be finished. She can operate a pending 'file' – holding over for the next day those tasks which are non-urgent (the ironing, cleaning the hamster cage out, applying for family passports).

She could remember too that FCEOs don't do everything – part of their role is smart delegation. That might be handing over paperwork to Sarah, who can sort through it on a Saturday morning, or getting the children to clean out pet cages as they grow old enough.

One task worth addressing as FCEO is overall morale as that comes from the top. It's often said that all you need for happy children is a happy mother. Certainly, if Monica is relaxed and receptive to all the needs of the family – including Sarah – the household mood will be easier. It's not her responsibility to make everyone happy, but she could embrace being the linchpin. So that means making time to have fun with Sarah as well as the children.

Draw the Line: *there's a nice paradox and neat bonus that the more boundaries you carefully construct and maintain, the more extra time you will create. This is something you will notice over and over as you work through the book and lay down your boundaries.*

FCEO working hours

Every couple with young children at home will recognise the 'handover flashpoint'. This is the moment when you and your partner – like two volatile chemicals – are most likely to meet and combust. The time it's most likely to happen is when both partners are tired, at the end of the day.

Both are worn down and full of the issues of their own day, looking for a bit of sympathy and support. The out-of-the-home worker may be hoping to be handed a cup of tea or a gin and tonic (in a stereotypical way), while the on-duty parent may be craving the chance to hand over the children instead. Both are experiencing the feeling of 'I just need a break'.

So how can this classic conundrum be eased to the satisfaction of both?

Pick a moment when you and your partner are relaxed and have uninterrupted time to establish the boundaries around this flashpoint. Listen to each other to understand just why resentment is flaring. How can you come together as a team?

For some couples, dividing the week can work so the FCEO knows that on Thursdays and Fridays he/she will be in charge, but in the early part of the week, they can rely on help from the other. Other couples may find this very tricky but while negotiation can show up some reluctance in one party to change, it doesn't mean that the change is wrong.

Divide tasks differently – the outside parent needs to be helped back into the team rather than forced. Perhaps that means they are responsible for bathtime later, or bedtime. Perhaps they can offer to be parent-in-charge on Saturday mornings.

Alternatively, why not reframe the 'handover flashpoint' as a 'family point' instead – so it's the moment which marks the end of everyone's working day and both parents share children and chores from this point on? The coming home becomes the coming together.

So now, how does it feel to run the company?

You may understand better now how vital your role is within the family unit – if you start taking it seriously, others will follow. A good FCEO respects themselves and is able to operate as an Adult, with self-respect engendering more external respect: a virtuous circle.

The Winner's Triangle

Earlier in this section we introduced you to the Drama Triangle and explained how understanding your position in relation to others could inform your decisions and actions. But there is another way of explaining how to achieve a better balance.

This is called the 'Winner's Triangle' – a theory developed by Australian psychotherapist Acey Choy.

To move across from the Drama Triangle to the Winner's Triangle, we look at each role and change it. So, draw your upside-down Drama Triangle again in your Learning Journal. Now, cross out the

'P' in the top left corner and and write 'A'. In the right-hand corner, cross out 'R' and write 'C'. And at the bottom of the triangle, cross out the 'V' and write 'V' again – in a different colour.

How Persecutor (P) Becomes Assertive (A)

The major difference between these positions is that in the Winner's Triangle, empathy is present. We claim our place on the Winner's Triangle when we are Assertive with empathy. This might mean that even if we believe we have a brilliant solution for someone else's problem, we remain aware of the impact we are having on them when we offer or suggest it. We pick up if they look uncomfortable; we ask their opinion on our idea rather than dictate it.

Might this be seen as weakness? Perhaps to someone who is deeply ensconced in a Persecutor role.

Think of Josef Stalin and his absolute belief that only he could make decisions for the good of his country and that these decisions did not need or involve empathy. He said: 'You cannot make a revolution with silk gloves.'

Who would really admire that as a philosophy to live by? Not everyone in your life may be a Russian dictator (or feel like it) but sometimes it can help to see the most extreme position. Because in this book, we are talking about building healthy relationships between equals, not game-playing unequal ones. And part of this means accepting that our opinions and habits do not have to be forced on to others to be valid, but nor need they be constantly swayed by others. It also means we can say what we want but not push purely for that want.

We're going to use an example of a possible trip to the cinema as a way of showing how you can alter your position, moving from Drama Triangle to Winner's Triangle, whether you start as a Persecutor, Rescuer, or Victim.

The cinema scenario

You as Persecutor: 'We're free this evening, I'm going to book tickets for that film.'

Partner/friend response: 'I'm not feeling great.'

A Persecutor reply might be to push them into going or sulk, e.g. 'You're always tired. We never do what I want.'

Or:

You as Assertive (given with empathy): 'Oh, I'm sorry to hear that. Let's stay in. But I would like to book tickets for the weekend.'

Can you see how the above response keeps communication going? No one loses out so the relationship stays more equal.

How Rescuer (R) becomes Caring (C)

As we've explained, caring for yourself first (remember the airplane oxygen mask) is central to setting good boundaries with others. So, moving to a Caring position is crucial before you decide how much to help others.

Don't forget the first step of moving from Rescuer to Caring is to consider how you are feeling. A Rescuer always worries about the other person's feelings first. Do you feel uncomfortable at this thought? This demonstrates that your favoured position is normally as a Rescuer. And indeed some Rescuers argue that it is selfish to care for yourself first. Or there might be a fear of no one liking you if you stop rescuing. But this is about a new healthy way to be in a relationship with others. Remember, it is called the Winner's Triangle – everybody wins.

Let's consider that dialogue we used above when you feel driven to Rescue.

The cinema scenario

Partner/friend says: 'I'd like to go and see that film this evening.'

Rescuer response (despite feeling tired): 'Oh yes, I know you've been waiting to see it.'

Or:

Caring response: 'Actually, I'm feeling tired. I'd like to go but it would need to be another day.'

How Victim (V) becomes Vulnerability (V)

What is your immediate response to the word vulnerability? Write it down in your Learning Journal.

One common response is fear – and that is a good thing to notice. We need to be aware of our own vulnerability and protect it.

When we are in the Victim place, our vulnerability is clearly displayed and invites Rescuing or Persecuting. But a healthy vulnerability is about us caring for ourselves; it is about deciding who you show your vulnerability to. It's not a free-for-all.

And showing your vulnerability is a really important part of a relationship and something a Rescuer or Persecutor would not be able to do. It's about being Vulnerable to those you are close to – and letting them in.

People have different reasons for feeling vulnerable. These could be health-related – like a long-term illness or phobia. It can be related to fear, grief, or loss, so we need to be careful to whom we open up. Because there are risks attached to exposing our vulnerabilities – as we have seen in the Drama Triangle – when they are all laid bare to Rescuers and Persecutors.

But in the healthy Winner's Triangle, it is safer to show Vulnerability, as those who are Assertive and Caring will not take advantage of our honesty.

A note of warning: don't rush into showing your Vulnerability before you have established a safe relationship. Some people will never leave the Drama Triangle. You may have to disentangle yourself from those relationships altogether. Bear in mind this is self-care, not trying to save the world. To successfully stay on the Winner's Triangle you need to establish everyone's Caring, Vulnerable and Assertive credentials before you open up your vulnerability. This is because when we move to the Winner's Triangle, there is always a knock-on effect on relationships; that impact will vary. Some may find it a surprise you are caring for yourself, say, and not rescuing them anymore. But they may be pleased to see you are caring for yourself. This would indicate a healthy relationship, where you could show your Vulnerability.

If, however, the person you are in a relationship with does not want to relinquish their Persecutor or Rescuer role, it wouldn't be wise or healthy to become Vulnerable with them as they may take advantage of your openness to draw you back on to the Drama Triangle.

You may be surprised at who you can be Vulnerable with. Jennie has known clients who have learnt that they cannot be Vulnerable with their mothers, for example, without the relationship becoming dramatic again. However, they have learnt there may be a friend or other family member who is comfortable with their Vulnerability and will not use it for their own emotional needs.

The cinema scenario

Partner/friend says: 'I'd like to go and see that film this evening.'

Victim says: 'Do we have to go to the cinema tonight? I can't really afford it.'

Partner/friend (in Persecutor) says: 'That's because you went out so much at the weekend without me.'

Victim: 'Oh very well then, I'll find a way.' (Adds fee to credit card bill.)

Or:

Vulnerable alternative: 'Yes, you are right, and because of that I am going to be more careful this week. We could have a nice evening at home and make a plan to see the film together next weekend.'

> 'So many people prefer to live in drama because it's comfortable. It's like someone staying in a bad marriage or relationship – it's actually easier to stay because they know what to expect every day, versus leaving and not knowing what to expect.'
>
> ELLEN DEGENERES

Conclusion

Now you have worked through the second Step of the book, you will have progressed in your ability to understand how to use boundaries, particularly in the work environment.

Think about your current workplace: is there one colleague, boss, or issue with the environment you would like to improve? How can you use what you have learnt in this step to facilitate that change? Make some notes in your Learning Journal.

Step Two Summary:

- Establishing healthy boundaries is key to work–life balance.
- Don't be poisoned by a toxic workplace.
- When we Rescue others there is always a cost to ourself.
- A healthy self-boundary does not disrespect others.
- The bully/bullied dynamic affects all and can leak beyond the workplace into home life.
- Like a good driver, be aware of your surroundings and those in it.
- Not every relationship can be saved – or needs to be.
- Choose your friends/lovers from among your colleagues with care.
- Do put a boundary around work time.
- If you are the FCEO, take your role seriously – and others will follow.

STEP THREE:

LOVE AND INTIMACY

'I'm not a romantic ... But even I concede that the heart does not exist solely for the purpose of pumping blood.'

THE DOWAGER COUNTESS OF CRAWLEY, *DOWNTON ABBEY*

In Step Three, we're going to explore how to use boundaries in your most intimate relationships, drawing on your past experiences to help you learn. It's worth noting that intimacy covers not just our sexual relationships but those we establish with friends and even with people we actively dislike.

We'll look at making the most of the partner relationship you have at present, plus how to approach and survive a break up and how to look for new love in a confident and secure way. There will also be advice on your close friendships and some discussion on navigating relationships which seem more based on hate than love.

Exploring the Love Myth

There are few biological entities with the curious desire to team up once and for life: swans, prairie vole, French angelfish – and, of course, (most) humans. Apart from that desire, we don't have much else in common as species. Certainly, it's unlikely that voles invest as heavily in the concept of the One True Love as we humans do.

Because from the moment humans first start listening to bedtime stories – delivered from the mouths of those nearest (and sometimes dearest), we are imbued with messaging based heavily around the concept of the search for The One, regardless of the immediate role models we see. Think of fairytales like *Sleeping Beauty* and *Cinderella*, or films such as *Shrek* or the young penguins in *Happy Feet*. The messaging is often deliberately non-specific, yet carries with it the subliminal call that love is heterosexual, monogamous and status-linked.

In Disney's *Enchanted* – a film that sent up those classic Disneyfied dreams of old – the heroine, Giselle, sings at the start of finding a true love's kiss – and naturally of a prince she hopes comes with that. To find him, Giselle goes on a magical journey to New York, and learns *en route* that a prince who looks good on paper may not necessarily be the right match for her, once she has got to know him properly. The film ends up with Giselle finding a 'prince' but this one is a single dad, supports her professional ambitions to open a fashion company and doesn't wear a doublet and hose.

But Disney can't quite let go of the dream: Giselle's perfect match is a male who is handsome and a corporate New York lawyer with a great flat. It seems even when pop culture chooses to acknowledge the reality of modern romance we cannot escape the idea that part of our whole purpose is finding a True Romanticised Heterosexual Love.

So where do boundaries come into this?

This love myth sets us all up to fail as couples because it encourages the idea of love with no boundaries, or with you and your loved one in a bubble behind a joint boundary. In reality, many of us feel like this in the first heady days of love or lust. We discover we like the same films, the same foods, share a sense of humour and are fascinated by each other's words or thoughts. We mirror each other as our relationship develops in intensity.

However, we all know the moment inevitably arrives for the first disagreement. You might learn that the other does not enjoy a sport you do. They might confess they have never really shared your passion for Coldplay but wanted to see you happy. This can cause irritation, disillusionment, or may even cause you to break up.

If your relationship survives this flashpoint it is the moment when you could start to develop healthy boundaries which will make you sustainable as a couple in the long term. Rather than a difference of opinion or taste marking the end of a partnership, it can be a useful signal that your relationship is ready for some appraisal and healthy growth.

In some ways this is similar to a child realising that their parent is not perfect and indeed that they hold some different views. Ideally – in a good-enough parent-child relationship – the parent allows the flexible skin-like boundary to grow with their own view and tolerate being perceived as not perfect. That relationship grows with the child growing. For a parent, the child's new perception of them as imperfect can feel like a rejection – after all, it's nice to be regarded as perfect – and in a partner relationship, one half may feel equally snubbed. But actually it's a healthy stage in the development of any relationship. The risk of not acknowledging this moment and the positive developments it brings is that each half of the relationship – suddenly disillusioned with the fall from grace – may retreat to their bunkers or build inflexible walls around themselves (not permeable boundaries) and survey each other warily from behind these barriers. In doing this, the couples both remain rooted in their own beliefs about the relationship and what is wrong with it.

By initially exploring where these barriers started to be built and what each partner needs to be able to come out from behind their own fortress, we begin the process of creating a new boundary around the relationship and what is necessary within that to help it to prosper.

We all get entrenched in our own beliefs about what is wrong with a relationship. This isn't always about blaming the other; sometimes one will hold on to the blame, or feel they are at fault, when in fact the landscape of separateness has often been jointly created. So, one partner might be convinced they are the naturally 'impatient' one – perhaps having been told that. Then, if arguments develop about punctuality, they instinctively take the blame thereby letting the other off scot-free for being a poor timekeeper.

Now, we're going to look at the way relationships and love develop from the earliest age. But first, remember Step One. Think about your self-boundaries again, as these are not to be lost when it comes to entering and enjoying intimate relationships with others.

Draw the Line: *a self-boundary is knowing how much to give to another while maintaining care for yourself.*

LOVE AUDIT

This section is designed to help you to analyse your past behaviour and relationships so that you can look at your current situation with a considered view. We're going to start with an exercise.

EXERCISE: The Cost of Love

Let's look back at the stages of relationships which have got you to here – whether 'here' is single, dating, married, divorced, bereaved, in a happy or unhappy way. This exercise is going to require a little time and space to complete. We'd encourage you to set aside a moment when you can really think about the following questions, making notes of your answers in your Learning Journal. Remember, there are no right or wrong answers, just your personal experiences.

Consider and make a note of each of the following:

- Have you ever considered how attached you feel to your original care-givers? We're not looking here at a simple statement like, 'Oh yes, I loved Mum and she loved me.' It's time to dig a bit deeper. So, think about what that love meant and how it was expressed. Do you recall being cuddled as a child? Did that physical affection stop when you reached a certain age or are your family still demonstrative in their love? If you can't remember, what you know of your parents in later years may help you answer that question.

- Who was your first crush, pre-puberty? This could be the girl or boy next door or it might be the singer from a teen pop group.

- Let's look at teen love: were you the object of a crush? Did you feel popular at school in general? Did you feel isolated? Would your friends have described you as attractive, clever, sporty, cute, or idolised you in any sense? Did you get Valentine's Day cards (not from your sympathetic family)?

- Do you recall your first foray into real dating – and was it happy? Did you feel pressurised into behaviour you weren't ready for? Were you happy to watch from the sidelines, comfortable in your own timeframe? Did you have a reputation – positive or negative? Were you struggling with your sexuality or sense of gender? Did you have a holiday romance? Did your parents know any of this?

- Who was your first serious love – and are you still with them? If not, were they the one that 'got away'? Did you have a faithful relationship? Were you hurt or disappointed when it came to

an end, or did you initiate the break up? And were you fair in
your own behaviour (looking back honestly)?

- Have you ever checked up on them or anyone else since online?
  Have you thought of initiating contact? Are past loves casting
  a shadow over your present life as well as your love life?
- Would your friends describe you as happy in love overall, or
  unhappy?
- Where are you now with your sexuality? Are you confident?
  Unsure? Or experimenting?
- If single, are you looking for love, licking your wounds, or gener-
  ally fearful?
- If in a couple, are you centred and secure, worried, or resentful?

Your answers to these questions will help you as we explore
how to set down some boundaries in regard to your current or
future relationships and how to draw some lines regarding the
past, if necessary.

In the next sections we will help you to understand current and
past relationships and examine how to stay in love and improve
the existing relationship you have. We will also cover what happens
when it is time to make an exit as comfortably as possible, if staying
really doesn't make any sense anymore, and in Looking for Love,
we cover dating.

   Lastly, we will look at how the same boundaries are applicable
in those non-intimate relationships with your friends and peers.

Love Limits

We're going to ask you to start by helping you analyse your current relationship, with a visualisation.*

Take a moment and close your eyes. Inhale a few deep breaths and settle yourself.

Picture yourself at a time when you were in your first grown-up sexual relationship.

Now place yourself in a room you feel comfortable in. And bring in your past loved one.

Start picturing what boundary lies between you – is it opaque or translucent, small or large, made of recognisable material and who has control of the boundary? Is ownership of the boundary shared or singular and does that change according to time or events or needs (such as one of you suffering a bereavement and feeling vulnerable)? Is the boundary visible to others? Would the boundary look the same from either side? Or is the boundary around the two of you excluding all others (as if you are in a bubble, which is not uncommon with a first love – the intensity can be all-consuming)?

Looking back, does the situation seem happy and comfortable?

---

* Listen to this visualisation exercise for free on Soundcloud at bit.ly/boundary-visualisation

Could you be looking through rose-tinted glasses or when you now recall the relationship does it make you shudder?

Come back out of your picture and write/draw all of that in your Learning Journal.

Now, let's remind ourselves what a healthy boundary is; you may remember we compared it to the natural layers of skin – dense enough to protect and contain us, but flexible to allow for necessary movement. Do you think that is true of the boundary that you have drawn for this past relationship?

> *'You can clutch the past so tightly to your chest that it leaves your arm too full to embrace the present.'*
>
> JAN GLIDEWELL

Some people may have been able to move on from first loves with ease and a natural sense of progress, be that experience good, bad, or indifferent. Others may find the first love sets a tone or standard they struggle to replicate. You may not realise how common it is to carry the baggage of even a good relationship into the next.

Draw the Line: *the first emotional boundary you need to check is that which separates old and new love.*

CASE HISTORY

James, a 47-year-old accountant, initially contacted Jennie to make an appointment for a couples' assessment. When the date came, he turned up alone.

James said his wife had refused to come and he had been trying to get them to see someone for years. Now he had decided to have individual therapy to help find a way forward.

He was very focused on his unhappiness in the relationship though from the outside most would say it looked like he was part of a successful functioning family. What friends couldn't see – but were beginning to pick up – was that his wife had lost interest in the marriage and he was becoming lonely.

He told Jennie that he had idly started looking up old friends, including ex-girlfriends, online – and that one of them had then got in touch. Reminded of happier, younger days, he was minded to meet up.

Jennie asked him to describe their relationship from the time and what gave him such fond memories. He talked about a passionate love affair where he had been idolised, a stark contrast to the way he felt his wife viewed him. It was also a time when he was part of a group of friends and felt he mattered to them. Clearly, there was a desire to enjoy that kind of life again.

However, Jennie pointed out the danger in trying to recreate the past. If he met up with his old flame, would his wife find out? What might she do? How would he feel if she divorced him on the grounds of adultery? How would his children and current friends view him? Could he not learn from the positive elements of that first relationship without having to relive it?

Looking at his dilemma through the Drama Triangle, James could see he had become a Victim in his current relationship. If he pursued the meeting and it was found out, he would then be seen as the Persecutor by his wife. How could they get off the Drama Triangle and on to the Winner's Triangle?

James could clearly see this and realised that rather than avoiding the difficult issues, he needed to be direct with his wife and talk about his unhappiness. Through this whole process, he had become aware of how unhappy he was and that he needn't hold all the blame.

So what can we learn from James's story? He had lost sight of who he was and stopped listening to himself. Thinking back to the debating table, the controlling Parental voice had been telling him to put up and shut up, the caring side of him was focusing on his actual children (nothing wrong with that but it meant he had forgotten to care for himself), but the youngest rebellious part of himself had had enough – hence the Facebook temptation.

Through talking to Jennie, he learnt to take account of all of himself and his feelings. Clearly, he needed to readjust the relationship with himself. By the time James came to see Jennie his marriage was probably over, which is a shame because many people only realise their relationship is in trouble when it is too late. Yet in recognising that there are problems developing (or potentially developing) early intervention can save quite a lot of relationships.

James missed the early signs, but you don't have to. This is a lesson you can take from past relationships. But how else can you improve or even save the relationship you have, bringing it into a state of healthy balance?

EXERCISE: Balancing Your Current Relationship

In Step One, we looked at how to achieve balance for yourself in your own mind. Now, you have to maintain that status quo while finding an equitable state with another (who will also be dealing with their own internal balance, we hope).

To help you work out if your relationship is well-balanced, try to answer the following questions, noting down your answers in your Learning Journal:

Values and beliefs: do or don't you share political, religious and cultural values? If you don't, is that a source of conflict or do you enjoy the debate?

Money: if you are living together, do you have similar or different views on how the house works? Is money a difficulty – does one have more control over it (or the topic in general)? Do you complain about not being in control, but are secretly relieved?

Nurture: do you nurture each other evenly? Or is one half the carer and the other either cared for or dismissive of care?

Class: are you aware of the 'social hierarchy' – either individually or as a couple? Was the similarity or difference part of the attraction?

Fun: is this a part of your relationship and does one of you take more responsibility for it? Do you ever feel that fun is now something you do with your children, not with each other?

Emotions: is it OK for both of you to be emotional – or does one of you have ownership of being emotional?

Envy/competitiveness: where do you compete? Do you have a strategy for dealing with this? Whose needs take priority?

Spark: can you look at your other half and recapture or remember that moment or spark when you first met?

Sexual intimacy: do you still make love?

Non-sexual intimacy: do you ever hold hands or stroke your partner's back as you pass?

Problem-solving: how do you solve problems? Are you able to stay on subject or do you both start bringing in old grievances?

Hopefully, these questions will have prompted you to look at your relationship in a new way. But your answers may have felt uncomfortable at times. These are the flashpoints which suggest your relationship is not as well-balanced as it could be.

For example, did the idea of who does the caring chime with you? Sometimes we think we are nurturing the other, but perhaps missing the mark a little. So, your partner might offer you a cup of tea when you get in from work, but what you really want is their full attention for five minutes so you can download your day. Tea is nice, but doesn't hit this spot.

Draw the Line: *listen to your partner and don't believe you can read their mind/feelings.*

This means talking about one issue at a time and if either partner starts 'archiving' (i.e. pulling in the past 'but last month you said/did . . .') you press a pause button for time out and come back to it later. Don't rush to get a relationship on a better footing; pace, space and time will aid the process.

Silver splitters

The number of older people getting divorced is on the rise. When couples are faced with an empty nest, it can seem an ideal time to recapture the fun energy in a relationship. You often hear couples saying this will be their chance to take up new hobbies together, such as salsa dancing. A chance to have fun again. But beware of waiting until it's too little too late; the rising divorce rates in the over-60s (and Jennie's own practice experience) reveal that looking to re-energise a stale relationship at this point is shutting the stable door after the horse has bolted.

It's harder to breathe life into a relationship worn out and weary than it is to take a preventative approach where you aim to inject in a little fun constantly along the way.

So many couples who have put their need for fun together aside while the children are growing up think they can pick up the reins at any time. Sadly, experience has shown time and again that for at least one partner, fun is not something that can be picked up at will.

Staying In Love

This is the area which concerns Jennie's clients most often. Having accepted there is a problem of some sort, how does a couple move past diagnosis towards an improved 'healthier' relationship and how can boundaries help with this?

All relationships need attention and tweaking every so often. Admitting this to yourself is not a sign the relationship is past saving or that you have both given up on each other.

Draw the Line: *accepting your relationship can benefit from scrutiny, consideration and spring cleaning is a sign of a healthy attitude to love.*

BRING IN THE BOUNDARIES:

Your Current Relationship Plan

Having answered the questions on the previous section, you may look at your own relationship and find one of these three classic dynamics at work: 'Parent and Child', 'Always Grown-ups', or 'In the Playground'.

Parent and Child

A familiar dynamic might be one partner taking on a Parent-style role and the other falls into a Child position.

Think of sensible lawyer Mark Darcy and hapless Bridget Jones in *Bridget Jones's Diary*; he cannot help disapproving of her antics, she cannot help provoking him.

As Bridget found out, Mark was quite capable of being supportive (behaving in a nurturing fashion and thinking for both of them) but didn't know how to relax. He wasn't trying to offend her, however. And he did enjoy her fun, spontaneous behaviour cheering up his life.

So your partner may be more in control but it doesn't necessarily mean they are older or critical. You may bring youthful energy into the relationship, but they will still be driving it. Both of you are responsible for causing any tension or faults.

Those in a relationship that is very Parent-Child usually display weaknesses in the other direction, e.g. the Parent might struggle with spontaneous gestures, the Child may equally not contribute much nurturing or leading. This imbalance in a relationship is often part of its initial attraction as together they make up for each other's deficiencies – 'opposites attract' we say. But over time, what appealed initially can become a source of frustration as one partner feels they always have to do the planning, present-buying, or household administration, while the other resents feeling patronised.

This could sound like:

'You don't respect my opinion.'

'Why can't you be more fun?'

'You think too much about money.'

'You don't take me seriously.'

'I have to do everything.'

'Someone has to be sensible around here.'

Couples need to think about this as a joint problem and therefore look to take equal responsibility. Start with one area which isn't too contentious. (Maybe avoid money as this has its own dynamic, which may skew the best intentions.)

Why not start with fun? If the spontaneous contact has gone, there is probably little fun, laughter, or jollity in your relationship – perhaps that behaviour was part of your past together, so what can be done to refresh that? Remember what you used to enjoy doing together – maybe take up a sport again as a couple, or join a theatre club.

And rather than it always being one person organising your free time as a couple, agree to share it. Each of you will organise something for you both to do. This could be weekly or every two months. The actual schedule doesn't matter, it's what works for you.

It's important that the other willingly participates in whatever is arranged. The more Parental partner may have lost the habit of organising fun so the Child-like partner must respect the effort involved and take part with good grace even if first attempts are not perfect. Likewise, the Parental partner must show willing even if they find themselves being asked to have fun in a way which stretches their self-boundary a little.

The Child-like partner should be respectful of how far this boundary can reach without causing distress and so should not take advantage of this exercise. Success will depend on goodwill and an understanding that neither party is 'winning'. This is a joint project.

Always grown-ups

Think of Bridget Jones's parents: Pamela temporarily leaves Bridget's father, Colin, and begins an affair with a shopping channel presenter named Julian.

Pamela explains her concerns about her husband to Bridget, pointing out she has spent thirty-five years cleaning her husband's house, washing his clothes and bringing up his children. 'And now it's the winter of my life,' she says, 'and I haven't actually got anything of my own.' She feels she has been left with no power, no career, no sexlife, in fact, no tangible life at all.

This dynamic can happen when life is busy and stressful; you both might have very demanding jobs. You work well as a team, keeping home together and bills paid, but equally you both work at weekends, work late, have little time for self or other. You have a shared strong work ethic and a shared aim that when you have worked enough and saved enough, life will start. But life needs to begin now.

Alternatively, this is the couple where one half is staying home to raise the children and in the process expending their caring, joyous energy on the younger members of the family rather than using it for fun with the other adult. Such a relationship may be cash-rich but is running out of oxygen. This often prompts the classic situation when one partner falls in love dramatically and moves on quickly, leaving the other half shocked and feeling they have been cheated literally of a future that was planned by both.

It sounds like:

'We may pass like ships in the night, but we both know where we are going.'

'We forfeit holidays now to pay off the mortgage early.'

'The children are OK.'

'Retirement will be our time.'

'We should be sensible; the time for romance is over.'

Each individual needs to start by reflecting on themselves. And really noticing what is missing; for example, how tired you are, or if you are not able to remember the last time you and your partner laughed together.

Can you see that the first problem is to do with yourself (tiredness; attitude to fun)? You need to establish a healthier internal balance and self-boundary and *then* think how to incorporate that boundary into the relationship. Get your own self in order before you work on the relationship.

Readdress what you need individually – this might be stepping away from the relationship (finding time for friends or playing tennis, for example), but then also making time together for something that is not so goal-driven.

Mortgages need to be paid and children reared, but remember why you got together initially – did you find each other to pair off and buy property, or did you fall in love and have fun?

Spontaneity is, of its nature, very difficult to prescribe but chances are your initial relationship was much more spur-of-the-moment, so ideally you want to capture a little of that again. This might mean planning a surprise; sharing something funny regularly (why not buy a box set of a comedy series that you both used to enjoy together?); or getting into a habit of exchanging jokes when you get home from work rather than problems.

In the playground

In *Bridget Jones's Diary*, this situation would be exemplified by Bridget's relationship with Daniel Cleaver – there is lots of fun but neither is taking responsibility for the relationship's future.

A number of relationships start this way – this dynamic is an important and healthy part of a relationship and the time described as the 'honeymoon period' (which can happen in any relationship at any age, even if you find your loved one at 75). You may hear friends lamenting that they 'wish they could go back to the honeymoon time', but it's natural to leave it behind as we take on responsibilities. We just need to make sure we don't lose track of it altogether.

We might recognise it in the couple who've been engaged for years – always talking of how, when they marry, they'll settle down properly. They may look as if they're behaving like this just because it's fun, but are they also shying away from responsibility and the need to look after themselves and each other, as well as the chance to let their relationship grow? Such couples may also not really want to get married (indeed to anyone) and this protects their single state.

Another element which may be familiar is an over-competitive tendency so that both partners like to play and to win at every aspect of their lives.

It may sound like:

'We're not ready to settle down just yet.'

'We don't want to turn into our parents.'

'We don't want to worry about a mortgage.'

'Children can wait.'

Like the others, this couple needs to look at their individual boundaries first and to establish how they are looking out at the world and whether it is in a healthy way.

This might mean accepting an underlying fear of commitment in one or both of you. Are you both distracting yourself from the reality of a relationship which just isn't working by constant holidays, moving home and buying pets? Is your frenzied social life – always with others, never alone – just a displacement activity to avoid breaking up?

Talk openly and honestly with each other about how you would feel if your social life dropped away altogether and you really had to face up to the future without distraction.

BRING IN THE BOUNDARIES:

Your Stay-in-Love Plan

The following pointers will help you strengthen your current relationship. Pick out those that speak to you most and make a note in your Learning Journal. You may want to also write down your partner's reaction to any of these changes. Set a reminder on your phone or in your diary to revisit this section in three months' time. What changes have been effective and lasting? What could you do differently?

- Don't rely on the relationship for all your needs to be met. That can put too much pressure on the best relationship. If you love cycling and your partner loathes it, it is more than OK to go off and follow your passion. Indeed, it is essential. Part of a healthy relationship is what we do outside, it which then brings back a positive energy to a relationship.
- Take shared responsibility for the day-to-day running of your lives. If one of you is a good cook and the other is good at washing up, that is a shared deal – you don't need to divide out every individual task.
- Agree to have fun even if sometimes it is more to one person's taste than the other. It's lovely to see your partner having a

good time and don't forget that laughter is contagious. Share responsibility for time out together. Take turns in organising it.

- Respect your partner and show it. From saying thank you and meaning it, to not shaming them in front of other people. They might have really upset you but don't let the world know that. Don't eye roll. Respect the relationship – that's the boundary.
- When in doubt, press the pause button and do what you need to do to get back into a thoughtful place.
- Have regular meeting points in the day – for example, a meal, coffee, or a phone conversation and regular joint bedtime.

Time to talk?

Here are some tips on starting a conversation about your relationship. Think tone and pace. Don't be patronising or pleading, be reasonable and calm.

- You might start with: 'I have been considering/thinking about this.' (Shows that this is not a spur-of-the-moment thought.)
- Bring up the areas that you are content with first. If you can pace it, do. Ask your partner if they are content with those areas too. Your partner may be urging you onwards to the problem they know is coming. Keep what you want them to hear short.
- Alert them to the problem you have – whether it is lack of fun, or that you feel they're too judgemental. Give them space to consider this. You may decide to ask if they want to come back the next day. It is tempting to want an instant response, but taking something seriously is about giving it time.
- Do listen properly to what you're hearing; if you want this to be successful, don't make your partner take the blame for everything that is not perfect between you.

Naming Your Love

What do you call the person you love?

How about: my wife, my husband, my partner, missus, my other half, my soulmate, my significant other, my better half, my lover, she who must be obeyed, The Boss, her indoors, him outdoors, my man, the wife, hubby, sweetie, sweetheart, pumpkin, baby, darling, Mum, Dad, sweetie pie, baby doll, mon petit choux, love of my life, light of my life, angel, Daddy, dear, dearest, dearie, dear one, heart's desire, honeybun, honeybunch, lamb, jewel, pearl, precious, pet, Princess, Prince, my sweet, sugar, treasure, beautiful, true love, gem, saint, babe, buttercup, button, cherub, dumpling, little angel, little darling, little doll, number one, doll face, the Master, inamorato, my passion, honey bunny, dreamboat, man of my dreams, woman of my dreams, dream guy, dream girl, lady love, lovebird, main man, main woman, paramour, patootie, squeeze, steady, stud muffin, sugar daddy, sugar momma, my cougar, my toy boy, snookums, beautiful flower, sugar lips, hot stuff, hottie, Casanova, Don Juan, lothario, beau, belle, sugar plum, hero, Venus, goddess, The Guvnor, my enchantment, gorgeous, friend with benefits, booty call, fuck buddy, bang buddy, partner, coquette? Or do you even use the more archaic form in front of others of Mrs and Mr, or His Lordship and Her Ladyship …

Or perhaps you even use their given name? But however you regularly describe that person you are in an intimate relationship with is very revealing.

Let's start at the beginning. If you have been in a relationship for a fair amount of time, what did you call your partner in the first heady days and how do you refer to them now? Has honeybun been replaced by The Boss? Can you see that the softness and easy affection has been replaced with a label – which has significant connotations?

Take a moment to consider when this change happened. Did it

coincide with events such as the formalising of your relationship, or the arrival of a child? Practical changes in circumstances (e.g. job loss or illness or bereavement) could also trigger a name change in response to a real role change.

Perhaps that label 'The Boss' was earned by a partner who took charge at a time of uncertainty and is respectful. However, it could also be the manifestation of a power shift in the relationship, uncomfortable or not, taking it to more of a Parent-Child place.

With the arrival of children, have you swapped given names for the ubiquitous Mum and Dad, and how does that affect your relationship when you are away from them (especially when having sex)?

Notice what you call yourself – do you refer to yourself in the third person? For example, 'Mummy says …' or 'Granny says …'? Can you see that this is talking from a role, rather than from yourself?

BRING IN THE BOUNDARIES:

Your Name Plan

Let's start with the role-defining nomenclature – do you call yourself or allow others to call you by your role, not your name? Typically 'Mum' or 'Dad' (but see how easy it is to let that spread into describing other organisational roles such as The Boss or The Guvnor).

Let's take the example of calling yourself 'mum'. It might be that it feels nice – it is an important role, it may have been a hard-won role, so it's a verbal medal of achievement. But at what point do you lose your sense of self within that?

This is where boundaries play their part. There may be a positive place to enjoy the name 'Mum', but could there be a boundary around when you do that? Might the cut-off time be when the children go to bed and you can revert to being 'Jane', or however you might want to think of yourself? In setting the boundary around time with children being 'Mum' and time without children being you will aid your relationship with yourself and a partner. It helps to re-establish what the two of you were when you first connected as individuals not as parents.

Here, we are talking about a flexible boundary that supports all your relationships. It's worth also noting that when out for drinks with friends, what is the impact on yourself and your friends (not all of whom may have children) of calling yourself or allowing yourself to be called 'Mummy'? Are you perhaps enjoying the status the word 'Mummy' brings without considering the effect of its power on yourself and others?

Let's also consider the reasons why our partner might choose a name or nickname for us and if that is uncomfortable. Setting a boundary might ease the situation, even if it causes temporary turbulence. Better to be true to your 'self' than allowing internal resentment to grow.

CASE HISTORY

During a therapy session, 35-year-old Clare brought up a conversation she'd had with her now ex-husband which she couldn't seem to let go. She told Jennie that despite a long and openly affectionate relationship – which pre-marriage had included pet names used cheerfully in public – her husband had reacted oddly the day after they got married. He had, she recounted, told her off for using his nickname at the restaurant breakfast table and said he didn't feel such childish endearments were appropriate now they were a grown-up married couple.

He said they should call each other husband and wife – or by their first names – from now on in public and private. Clare was shocked, perhaps so much so that she didn't respond authentically and merely agreed glumly. Why, she asked Jennie, had this happened and was it part of the reason the marriage had broken down quite quickly?

This laying down of the law over names proved to be the first sign of how the marriage would unfold. For Jennie the key was Clare being in 'shock but not saying anything'. Jennie's hunch was that even though Clare expressed shock, was it actually familiar for her to be told what to do or not to do by a domineering other, which was why she was silenced and didn't respond?

The changing of the name in this instance was a tactic her ex-husband used for gaining control in the relationship.

This shows how powerful names are: we all know instinctively what we like to be called and by whom, but allowing others to define you verbally can be detrimental to a relationship as it may demonstrate an imbalance in power or diminish a sense of self. Adults choose their own name and ensure others use it.

But I don't want to be his mother!

We don't just assign ourselves roles, sometimes we have them thrust upon us.

For example, if your partner likes you calling him 'snuggles', do you feel unsettled by that? Does the relationship feel equal or do you feel like you are being placed in the position of mother?

Of course, there are times when we do need to nurture each other. But if one is always in the role of Parent and the other is in a Child role, as we spoke about back on page 180–1, frustration can build on both sides.

It is worth acknowledging that some men and women are looking for a dominant partner – which they might call their 'white knight in shining armour to rescue them' or their 'Mummy to nurture, protect and spoil them'. For some couples, names and definitions are part of the deal and both acknowledge and are comfortable with this.

Ask yourself, are you happy with the name your partner uses for you? If not, could you have a conversation about changing it? This is you using a self-boundary to protect yourself and what you feel is important.

Love Leaving

If you've digested the advice on the previous pages about improving the relationship you are in, you may have found it takes you to a different conclusion. A tougher one. Is it time to leave your lover?

Your Leaving Plan

The abusive relationship

'There's a phrase, "the elephant in the living room", which purports to describe what it's like to live with a drug addict, an alcoholic, an abuser. People outside such relationships will sometimes ask, "How could you let such a business go on for so many years? Didn't you see the elephant in the living room?" And it's so hard for anyone living in a more normal situation to understand the answer that comes closest to the truth; "I'm sorry, but it was there when I moved in. I didn't know it was an elephant; I thought it was part of the furniture." There comes an aha-moment for some folks – the lucky ones – when they suddenly recognize the difference.'

STEPHEN KING

Some relationships are unhealthy from the start, especially where one partner is controlling and dominant and the other has low self-esteem and is driven by a need to please others. It is not difficult for these relationships to become abusive in some way, physically or emotionally.

If this sounds like it could be your relationship (and you are the more fragile partner), you may feel that leaving the relationship is unthinkable, even if you acknowledge privately on some level that you are not happy.

Indeed, the idea of leaving reinforces the very feelings which are keeping you there – 'I am wrong', 'I deserve no more than this', 'I am not good enough', 'I couldn't survive on my own'. More than any other, the person who needs to please and has low self-esteem needs to strengthen their sense of self before they start to disentangle themselves from an abusive relationship. (Although this is good advice for all of us.) Certainly, you need your boundaries to be firm and clear as you begin to gain strength and to keep yourself safe.

BRING IN THE BOUNDARIES:

Your Plan for Ending an Abusive Relationship

- At this point, any individual counselling or psychotherapy will be useful to strengthen your sense of self (now may not be the time to start couples therapy; work on improving your self-esteem first).
- Often people in this situation will find themselves isolated, having been cut off or having cut themselves off from friends and family out of embarrassment or need, or at the insistence of the dominant partner. You need to reverse this situation and re-establish ties to those outside your immediate partnership.

The biggest step is going to be telling another person what you are going through – but once taken, it will get easier. And this applies for men and women. Try sending a text to a friend or relative: 'I'd like to get in touch' – and see how easily the door opens when you give it a gentle nudge.

- Stay safe. Transparency is not always the way forward. You do not need to apologise in advance or give any warning to the person you are leaving of your intentions, even though it may be your natural inclination to do so and the idea of not being open makes you feel uncomfortable.

- Only you can make a judgement on how lopsided your relation-ship is, but if you are in a relationship which already feels abusive, you may wish to leave before you open up any dialogue (even by text or e-mail) with the partner you want to leave. If your relationship is unhappy but your partner has shown no signs of physical/mental abuse, you can talk to them about leaving first. This may even help you decide if leaving is what you want to do. Even at this point, Jennie has known couples who not only have come back on track, but also get on a better track.

- What do you say? Adults do not have to give long reasons or excuses for their actions. So you do not have to explain to the nth degree – in fact it is important to allow space for your partner to engage with the experience themselves. So that means no 10-page letters of 'It's me, not you'. But equally, in most cases you, as an Adult, could consider and accept some degree of responsibility for the situation the relationship is in, even if just to yourself. That may be as simple as agreeing to be in a relationship at all to playing the sort of long-term mind games that ratchet up tension. When you do this, it can be a fight for control, which Jennie calls the 'Hand Slap game'. Each is trying to best the other, knowing the game to cause pain.

When do you say goodbye?

You may have been trying to have this conversation for years. How can you make it effective this time?

As suggested above, when talking about staying in a relationship, you still need to consider time, pace and tone and to make it clear that you have been considering this action for some time.

Think back to the Drama Triangle: it is important not to slip into the Persecutor role, or allow yourself to be derailed by a dramatic Victim, nor by slipping into the Rescuer role. Hold the boundary of what you want to happen. But don't expect this to be easy.

Set boundaries about the time and place for a conversation such as this. A good tip is to do it outside the house – on a walk perhaps (but not in the car, where one of you is concentrating on driving). Being in a different environment is helpful, it can feel safer. Even if you don't meet anyone, it encourages us more into Adult behaviour; plus the action of walking means our eyes don't have to meet, which lowers the risk of confrontation.

Say you want to talk and give it a time frame – walk for 15 minutes one way and 15 minutes back. Agree to give each other space afterwards to think about what has been said.

Again, if there is any risk of harm to yourself or if children are involved, find a safe place to go before divulging to your partner that you have separated from them.

If goodbye might be on the cards

If you are on the receiving end, many may begin by saying that they're surprised. But at heart, most will not be. A relationship that is unhappy for one can never be truly happy for the other.

So how to bear those six little words: 'I don't love you any more'?

First, try to think about what you're feeling (if anything – you

may be in shock and shut down emotionally). If you do feel
something – is it anger, disappointment, abandonment, or rage?

One thing that often happens in these circumstances is that your
mind will start to be flooded with a lot of questions. You may need
some time on your own to consider what you really need to ask.
You may feel the ground has been cut out from beneath you, so
why not carve out a new bit of turf giving you some control back?
Even though part of you wants to run away, do listen and think
hard about what you've learnt.

Were you really unaware of the problem? Self-honesty is crucial
to you now, either in mending a relationship and/or mending
your heart. For example, if you are told that you are too possessive,
think about what that might mean. Could you be attentive and
affectionate without smothering a partner? How would that work
in a new relationship?

There is an anonymous saying: 'Sad endings are but the next
happy beginning'. Whatever we want to be hearing when our
partner is discussing our relationship, there will always be a temptation to hide from a truth we don't want to hear, whether it's being
told we aren't fun anymore, or that we aren't loved any more. But
the true message is always there – just as the initiator has to own
saying it, we have to own hearing it.

You may have heard that you should grieve a week for every
month of your relationship and a month for every year to give
yourself time to heal, regardless of whether you initiated the separation or not. It's not a bad rule of thumb although some may need
less or more time.

The end of a relationship is a loss, a bereavement – not just of the
relationship but also the dreams and plans it evoked and inspired.
How do you feel about that length of recuperation; does it sound
sensible or does it interfere with your ideas of passion and 'falling

in love' being out of your control? If you do meet someone on the rebound, you might ask if the emotional element of your past relationship ended a lot earlier than expected, based on these time frames. We are not being prescriptive, but it's worth making sure you have thought through the end of one relationship before you begin the next.

Whatever your personal timeframe for romantic recovery, don't be unprepared for the lack of patience in others. Make sure you have a strong support network where you can return to your grief on occasion as necessary, even after you start a new relationship.

And don't be surprised if you still grieve if you were the active partner in the break up. It's OK to be sad to miss the good times and the once-positive future you had hoped for. Don't be too quick to paint yourself – or allow others to do so – as a villain. You may have been the hero of your story.

And whoever ends the relationship, remember you are in good company. There have been few humans who have not felt what you do now. Think of the words of seventeenth-century poet Sir John Suckling:

> *Why so pale and wan, fond lover?*
> *Prithee, why so pale?*
> *Will, when looking well can't move her,*
> *Looking ill prevail?*
> *Prithee, why so pale?*
> *Quit, quit for shame, this will not move;*
> *This cannot take her.*
> *If of herself she cannot love,*
> *Nothing can make her:*
> *The devil take her!*

Looking For Love

So, what if you are single long term, or newly separated and want to look for love in a way that has healthy boundaries from the start?

CASE HISTORY

Ellie, 29, came to see Jennie after her fiancé, David, was unfaithful, causing the breakdown of their relationship. She was nervous about dating again and wanted a little help exploring what had gone wrong in the past. She told Jennie that she felt she had done nothing wrong and her friends had all agreed so couldn't understand her own nerves.

After a session of talking, Jennie challenged that idea, asking Ellie to consider if David's last act of infidelity was wholly responsible for the breakdown of the relationship. Had Ellie been pushing for marriage at a hard pace, ignoring David's quietly expressed doubts, leaving him no way out except via the devastating and destructive statement of adultery?

This is an example of where friends can be very supportive but without Ellie really exploring her own part in the relationship, the risk would be that the same dynamic would recur in a future relationship.

BRING IN THE BOUNDARIES:

Your Dating Plan

Whether your last relationship ended as dramatically or was more of a damp squib, wouldn't it be better all round to work out what we want from a partner before we begin the relationship at all? This is not a shopping list for eye colour, hobbies, or income, it's more fundamental.

Imagine a dating agency where you typically quiz each other on likes, dislikes, hopes and fears. How often are both parties merely rehearsing trivial wishlists (favourite food/films/music) rather than opening up about what they truly value: characteristics such as reliability, openness and fidelity? Throw in some chemical attraction and this could describe the start of many modern relationships. You find yourself apparently bound together in a cocktail of attraction, shared hobbies and experiences.

At no point have you made it clear what you want from life, or really listened to what your partner wants. No wonder so many relationships later flounder, when one or other partner takes control and wrests the direction of the relationship in their favour. That's when cracks appear, which may or may not be solvable.

EXERCISE: Plan a Joint Future

Not every relationship will develop but there is usually a point where things could become more serious. That might be the moving-in point or the talking-about-the-future point. You might both believe that you have a shared view for the future, but does that really exist? And is it something you can intuit, or is it something that needs some honest questions and answers?

So, what if you were to ask each other these questions now?

Write the answers down in your Learning Journal – you can do this by yourself if you are presently single or if your partner is not ready to have this discussion.

It could help you establish what is important for you and your future:

- Where do I see myself in one year's time? How about in two, five, or ten years?
- Where does my partner/potential partner fit into that picture?
- What do I want for them? Would my answer to this surprise them?
- Am I ambitious for them – or is that tied to my own expectations of the relationship? For example, do I want them to be successful financially to take the pressure off me? Or do I see them in a supporting role for my career?
- Do we share ideas of what a family looks like?
- Are there shared values and beliefs? (This isn't necessarily a deal-breaker, but is important for future communications.)

What these questions do is avoid the biggest trap that couples have of believing that the other can read their mind. We can all have a romantic view, thinking: 'If they really knew me they would know what I want …' In fact the responsibility lies within ourselves. And in being brave enough to share that desire.

Look at the answers you have written down together. Or use a good friend to assess your responses if you are single. What surprises are there for you?

This is an exercise that is well worth repeating and revisiting over time, whether your current relationship lasts or not. We need to have healthy honest conversations with ourselves and others regularly.

Recording your answers and compiling this personal information is gathering the building material of your relationship boundaries. But don't imagine bricks and mortar going up. These are flexible walls, remember. This type of communication fosters a healthy transparent boundary of knowledge and understanding between the two of you. And potentially around the relationship as well.

Friends and Frenemies

Our ancestors certainly knew the value of friendship between like minds. Greek playwright and philosopher Euripides said: 'One loyal friend is worth ten thousand relatives.' But our forebears would be astonished no doubt at the way modern friendship has come to represent a better form of family for many, filling in the gaps, both physical and emotional, created by the effect of migration on households, whether international or merely miles away from the original village or town.

The rise of the leisured class has had its own impact too; pre-twentieth century, the working classes had little time for emotionally involved friendship. Even the upper classes knew that loyalty to family came before outsiders, however amusing those outsiders were. Closing ranks was a very real practice.

But in the twenty-first century we have come to revere, even worship, friendship. Our mates, chums, allies, pals are those who we meet at our first Saturday job, university or college, or backpacking through Thailand, on an intern programme in New York, or through a flat share in Leeds. These relationships are forged through mutual adversity – the awful boss, the bad break up, the time you got mugged and the creepy landlord. Billionaires have founded fortunes on our delight in amassing numerous virtual friends too, via Facebook, Twitter, Instagram, or online games.

We even judge each other on the ability to make large numbers of friends, or to be a good friend. Pop stars such as Taylor Swift and actors like Lena Dunham are valued by the way they are consistently loyal to their female buddies. Take That has made a fortune from the on-off bromance of singers Gary Barlow and Robbie Williams.

Indeed, Hollywood firmly drives the idea of the buddy movie, which has now deviated from chronicling the adventures of two good male friends (*Butch Cassidy and the Sundance Kid*), to two good female friends (*Thelma & Louise*), to entire swathes of men (*The Hangover*) and women (*Bridesmaids*). In the *Pitch Perfect* films, classic love interest plots were entirely secondary to the storylines around intense group friendships.

Perhaps the most pervasive influence has been from TV: think of the emotional dramas of *Thirtysomething*, the exuberance of *Seinfeld* and *Friends*, the false matey-ness of *The Office*, the home truths from *Girls,* the never-ending ties in *Cold Feet*.

Science is also fascinated by the idea of friendship as being a driver for longevity and good health. According to a New York study published in 2015 in the journal *Psychology of Ageing*, how we interact with friends in our twenties and thirties can predict our health in our fifties and sixties. Drawing on developmental theory, this 30-year prospective study assessed social activity at age 20 and age 30 and psychosocial outcomes (social integration, friendship quality, loneliness, depression and psychological wellbeing) at age 50. Results showed that the quantity (but not the quality) of social interactions at age 20 and the quality (but not the quantity) of social interactions at age 30 predict midlife psychosocial outcomes. Other studies link friendship in old age to better brain functioning, recovery from illness and longevity. Loneliness is a killer, doctors warn.

Inevitably this modern lionising of the 'friend' relationship can make them more important, trickier and even more complicated than some family situations. After all, the effect of placing friendship on such a pedestal is to throw loneliness into even sharper focus.

What if you don't have – or even want (and plenty are content with socialising with family or just a couple of selected friends) – a large social group?

Think of Pi, in the book *The Life of Pi*, so desperate for human company that he conjures up a tiger called Richard Parker into being just so he is not alone. 'Misery loves company,' he says. 'And madness calls it forth.' But also think about what Haruki Murakami says in the novel *Norwegian Wood*: 'Nobody likes being alone that much. I don't go out of my way to make friends, that's all. It just leads to disappointment.'

So can we learn to be 'better' at friendship, albeit at whatever level (facebook fanatic, old friends only, just me and my dog) inherently suits us as individuals?

Problems develop when there is a lack of healthy boundaries, as we are often not so careful in what we do or say around people who claim to be on our side. Ever posted something you felt was innocuous or obviously right on Facebook only to be surprised at adverse comments from people you considered friends in the modern sense of the word?

In this section, we'll point out some of the flashpoints for friendship tension and how to avoid them. Remember, it's not selfish to put your needs first when it comes to friends, it is healthy self-care.

Friends not lovers

It's been argued that we cannot be friends with those we might be sexually attracted to (regardless of whether that attraction is heterosexual or homosexual in nature). Famously, this was the plotline of *When Harry Met Sally*; and a study in 2001 by April

Bleske-Rechek of the University of Wisconsin seemed to back this up, at least from the male perspective. It found men were more physically and sexually attracted to their female friends and tended to overestimate how these women saw them.

Yet many of us cherish our male/female friends who we would swear blind not to be attracted to. And if there is an unspoken frisson does it matter anyway?

It might feel harmless but there are boundaries you should put in place and perhaps that you need to re-examine.

CASE HISTORY

James came to Jennie's practice to explore relationships. Part of their discussion revealed he had a close male friend, Tim, who was heterosexual, unlike James.

They had become close at university and Tim had supported James when he came out. James acknowledged that he had never had the slightest hint that Tim was interested in him and Tim was happy in his heterosexual relationship.

Even though they saw each other often with Tim's wife, James often felt down afterwards and couldn't understand why – was he just craving a marriage of his own?

Jennie began to notice the warmth of feeling James had for Tim – that it felt like more than friendship even though he wasn't really aware of this himself. The more they talked and explored the issue, the more James came to see that he didn't want just any marriage or relationship, he wanted to be with Tim.

Jennie suggested that this might also be a way of James actively avoiding entering other intimate relationships. His behaviour could partly have been about keeping himself safe, yet ironically it was causing him a lot of hurt.

In situations like this where one friend falls into unrequited love (and this may be something the object of love realises before the admirer), how can boundaries help?

The boundary to examine in this case is not the one between the friends, but the larger boundary that James has created around the two of them. This became apparent when Jennie enquired about his other friends and social life: James had been putting these on hold as he was always waiting for Tim to be available.

The answer was to slowly take down the boundary around them to preserve the friendship itself and give James the confidence to carry on.

Is this a time for a frank conversation? Probably not – the object of love may sense that frisson but will not have any idea of the overall impact he/she is having on their friend's life.

Instead, if James's experience sounds familiar, here are the steps to take, remembering this is about really being kind to you – but also involves a little tough self-love:

- Make a list of all the friends you can contact to go out with. Start planning events or trips with them, with no let-outs.
- Imagine yourself at a party with your unrequited love-friend and turn your body and head 180 degrees away to face the rest of the room and all the potential opportunities you have not been allowing yourself.
- Acknowledge that there may be a reason for your intense focus. If staying close to this person is somehow protecting you from risking a real relationship, can you ask what you are frightened of? Is this something you could pursue with a therapist in more detail?

These feelings may be familiar to us all from childhood when we fixated on someone like a pop star as it was a safe way to explore attraction. But it is important not to let that bleed into grown-up life.

Friends with benefits (FWB)

There is plenty of advice on how to have a FWB relationship – e.g. no dating, no staying over, minimal contact and a time limit on the whole affair. But the question this raises is – is this a friendship or is the reality, in fact, two people with a firm boundary around each of them (think brick wall) and no friendship? A FWB is not someone you would contact in a crisis or to share some good news.

As with James above, there is the chance one will fall in love or begin the FWB relationship hoping something will grow. Statistics show that a relationship evolving from this scenario is unlikely: a longitudinal study presented in 2014 at the Society for the Scientific Study of Sexuality found that only 15 per cent of FWBs grew into something more permanent. One in three FWBs ended with no ongoing contact or friendship.

In the film *Bridesmaids*, Annie has a FWB affair with Ted, who she wanted to be in a boyfriend-girlfriend relationship with. But he couldn't be clearer about his lack of interest in anything more.

When she asks him to go to a wedding party with her he says: 'I wouldn't want to make you explain what our relationship is to all those people. That would suck for you.' On the one occasion she asks for the friendship part to be active and calls him to collect her after her car breaks down, he turns up as he assumes it's for sex.

Calling a FWB relationship 'friends' is a misnomer. You could get lulled into a relationship which won't bring any of the advantages one ought to expect from a friendship. And when you take the word 'friend' out of it, what will you be left with?

And is it something that will benefit you and your self-esteem and self-care?

Making boundaries around facets of a FWB relationship is fairly meaningless if the greater boundary around caring for yourself is ignored. But as soon as you start to establish that boundary you may realise you want more than a FWB.

There will always be an 'ouch' for someone.

When friends don't match

There is always part of us which wants everyone we know to be like one big happy family – we want our family and friends to get on. We have to accept that this isn't always going to be the case.

EXERCISE: The Seating Plan

This exercise will help you consider how you negotiate the friendships you have and raise your awareness of who is really valuable to you and which friendships you feel obliged to be engaged with.

- To help think about this, draw or write in your Learning Journal the arrangements for a seating plan for a lavish party. There will be a top table, four tables at the front and then several rows further back, plus a table which is slightly to one side without great visibility.
- Who do you want to invite?
- How would you prioritise them?
- Would you group by association?
- Would you try to stage-manage friendships between groups?
- Would you consider no seating plan at all – and does that thought make you feel very uncomfortable?
- Who would you place on the far table – distant friends or people

you trust to understand someone has to sit there and who love you too much to be offended?

- Who would you place near you, even though you would prefer them to be as far away as possible?
- How do you navigate friends who don't like each other? Do you work at keeping them apart – and even consider having two parties so they don't meet?
- What if your partner doesn't like a friend – would you consider not inviting them?

If you have followed this exercise, you may have a clearer idea of who you value among your friends and who you feel obliged to value. Now is a good time to strengthen your self-boundary regarding the latter group. Interact with these friends if you want to, but not if you feel you 'should'.

Friends with theatrics (FWT)

Do you have a FWT relationship which thrives on drama and confrontation? While friends can give good guidance about new relationship partners – often when you are in the throes of intoxicating first love, which may leave you blind to faults – this advisory role can become unhealthy if a relationship becomes established of which they do not approve.

This may be caused by genuine concern: a friend could spot an abusive relationship developing and want to stay in contact to protect you or prevent harm. But it could also be triggered by a feeling they are losing power and influence over you.

CASE HISTORY

Jude and Lydia have been friends since school; their wider group now includes Megan.

Jude has got into the habit of complaining to Lydia about Megan's attitudes to finances. 'She's so petty about money, it's really upsetting me. You know how she is.' Then, having downloaded the complaints, Jude feels better and can spend time with Megan without appearing to worry and can't understand why Lydia remains antagonistic towards Megan.

Jude is Theatrical in her friendship style; she enjoys the drama of the moment (also known as gossip) without considering its longer-term impact on those around her.

So, how can you manage your friendships without playing them off against each other in this FWT way?

First, examine your own boundary to make sure you are not spicing up your worries or complaints with added drama. It's very human to have the odd moan to establish for yourself how important the issue is and whether you want to challenge it directly. This is using a friend as a sounding board and being prepared to hear some feedback – even if it challenges your views.

But 'moaning' for the sake of it is unfair to all three parties. In the Case History above, it is false care for Jude herself (she may feel a bit better at the time, but the problem isn't solved), it's not fair on Lydia, whose ear is being bent and whose temper may be incited, and it's not fair on Megan, who deserves the chance to defend herself or at least give some feedback.

Draw the Line: *if you hear yourself constantly complaining about a friend or partner, listen to that voice and examine the relationship. Perhaps it is time to move on from it.*

Do reread the Drama Triangle advice in the Step One summary on page 105. You may feel these scenarios are more familiar now when you apply them to your friends.

For example, when you consider your friends, you may realise that you yourself favour a certain starting position on the Drama Triangle with each of them.

Do you notice that with some you are pulled one way and with some another way – with one friend you are more the Rescuer, another you are the Victim?

With some relationships, you don't step on to the Drama Triangle at all, or if so, very fleetingly. And that will be a friendship which feels comfortable as there is no drama involved.

Think of a see-saw – all relationships take careful balance and you may at times be the one on the ground, at other times in the air. For example, one month you might be recovering from an operation leading to a close friend giving you plenty of practical support. Some time later, that same friend might want to cry on your shoulder. Both are giving and receiving, albeit at different times. This type of temporary imbalance is normal and doesn't mean you abandon the see-saw.

Do note that as we develop our own healthy boundaries in regard to friendships, partners and family, and as we move away from our favoured role on the Drama Triangle, some of those relationships will feel challenged by our change of behaviour (some might increase the drama in order to pull you back into the old way of relating). And some friendships might end.

One in, one out

As you learn to develop healthy boundaries with old friends and new, you may notice that there are some changes in personnel.

This may come about quite dramatically if you've been friends with someone and you have always been available (whether they wanted you or not) as the Rescuer, but have begun to see the imbalance in that relationship and have moved towards Caring for yourself and being more Assertive as a result. Then your Victim friend may move to Persecutor and become quite unpleasant. Or it may be a lot more subtle and you begin to notice you don't feel drawn to contact people so often, or they may not contact you (because you have redrawn your self-boundary in the friendship).

Over time, you will notice that the tenor of your friendships will change. Some may become 'frenemies' – an enemy disguised as a friend.

'It takes a great deal of bravery to stand up to our enemies, but just as much to stand up to our friends.'

– J.K. ROWLING, HARRY POTTER AND THE PHILOSOPHER'S STONE

How to tell who is a friend and who is a frenemy:

- Friends rejoice in your success; frenemies can't resist a barbed comment.
- Friends tell you when you are looking good; frenemies deal in back-handed compliments.
- Friends leave you feeling good if sometimes challenged; a night out with a frenemy can drain you of energy and leave you feeling down.
- Friends can be relied on; frenemies are slippery with their promises.
- You are never your best authentic self with a frenemy as you are always on guard or trying to please.
- Friends say sorry.
- Frenemies play to the audience and can be mocking while lacking empathy for the effect their barbed remarks are having.
- Frenimism is contagious, particularly in groups (which is where we give it the misleadingly innocuous term 'banter'); beware scoring laughs with mild or heavy insults.

BRING IN THE BOUNDARIES:

Your Friends and Frenemies Plan

Consider your friends with regard to the following points. Note down in your Learning Journal the names of those who seem relevant.

- Good friends are truthful even when it comes with risk. Who tells you the news you don't want to hear if you need to – whether that's about your partner, your job, or your family?
- Who presses your buttons by making throwaway comments which really hurt, or seems to provoke you into pressing theirs? The longer the friendship, the more you understand their weak

points as well as their strengths. Remember to use assertiveness with empathy. Don't be afraid to apologise.

- Give a little love. Who are your oldest friends? Do you take them for granted or feel that is how they treat you? Whose birthday do you want to remember, who do you never need to find time to catch up with and who always tells you how they feel and vice versa.

- We're all human and friends make mistakes. Who do you associate most with being forgiving and understanding? Who never holds a grudge? You can learn from these kind of friends. They never second-guess you and aren't afraid to spell things out. Do you feel relaxed around these people and if so, are they on your close friend list? Is their behaviour something you might like to model?

- We can learn from our good friends as well as enjoy their company. Not every friend has to be perfect, but when you look at the company you keep, does that make you feel happy and secure? Looking back at your list, is anyone missing? If so, how do they enhance your life?

Oversharing and Undersharing

Actor and writer Lena Dunham is probably the Queen of Openness. She admits that it's not just about getting worries off her chest: 'It's interesting to see how other people react to an oversharer.'

This is because oversharing isn't just exploring empathy.

It is:

- A trade of confidences used to build up a new relationship: 'I trust you with this secret, what can you share to beat that?'

- An opportunity to grandstand and hold the floor, grabbing attention. Difficult to stop unless someone steps into the spotlight with a more compelling story. Think of talent show competitors, each encouraged to reveal more and more emotional truths to garner public sympathy.
- A psychosocial tool to learn about or to control others in the group.

And the consequences may not always be in your control. Overshare inappropriately and you are leaving yourself open to others who may use that information in a way you would prefer them not to. You may blunt yourself to others using the same technique – think about the boyfriend who tells you about previous awful behaviour on a first date so that you cannot say you weren't warned later.

But undersharing is just as problematic and can lead to isolation. If no one knows you are really struggling with your job or university, how can anyone help? Undersharers classically help others but never ask for help themselves – they are fixed on the Rescuer position on the Drama Triangle.

So, how do you know if you are oversharing or undersharing? Let's look at some case histories.

CASE HISTORY

Eloise came to see Jennie to deal with the aftermath of her parents' divorce, something she hadn't discussed before as it had happened when she was very young. The struggle she had with openly reflecting on details of her life in therapy was a mirror of her interactions in everyday life with friends she would consider close. Jennie encouraged her to deal with this by opening up gradually in therapy, which helped her to be more relaxed and build stronger bonds with her friends at the same time. Jennie explained to her that sharing can be opening a door on a bit of your life and this type of sharing of yourself is part of the building of a friendship.

The oversharer

Some people will tell you their whole life history, including intimate details concerning sex, finances, sibling squabbles and opinions on everyone within their group, which may initially bond you to them. But this can begin to cause difficulties, particularly around meeting partners, when the oversharer has told you all about themself in advance. You may feel pressured into matching this level of personal detail when it makes you uncomfortable to do so at such an early stage.

So why do some people overshare? It's tied to an unconscious belief that in sharing every part of themselves and all of their vulnerabilities they will be more likeable.

Draw the Line: *for a healthy friendship, there needs to be a balance of caring from both sides, and acceptance of that care, plus fun and laughter and enjoyment of being in the Here and Now.*

Ghosting

Ghosting is the term used to describe when friends (or family or lovers) disappear from your life without warning and refuse to respond to pleas for contact or explanation. It can be hugely destabilising. But ask yourself, is it really always a surprise?

The idea that a friend could suddenly walk away from a close alliance without discussion causes consternation. It seems we can accept the idea that not all romantic relationships work, but that friendships must be retrievable, and moreover friendship itself is a kind of joint property – an association-in-common which cannot be dissolved unless both parties agree. The result is that the ghosted feel hurt and become vocal, and the ghostees go even more quiet. What's going on?

This classically occurs in a Rescuer-Victim friendship. The Rescuer may have begun to tire of the lack of emotional support from the Victim friend and has started to move to Persecutor by ghosting and leaving the relationship. As a result, the Victim has their belief confirmed – bad things do happen to them.

Meanwhile the Rescuer (who is moving to Persecutor) may be experiencing a familiar thought of 'I never get my needs met in relationships'.

Role play

Friendship makes some strange demands. Many of us fall into an amenable group only to discover that we have garnered roles: one may be the leader, another carries practical responsibility (arranging gatherings, collecting funds), a third may be the comedian, another the weary conscience and there is always a 'life and soul'. Do you know your role and are you happy with it?

'My daughter's my best friend'

Have you ever heard or said, 'My daughter's my best friend'? Or, 'I have such a good relationship with my daughter – we are like Besties.' Or, 'I am my daughter's best friend'?

Jennie has worked with a few mother-and-daughter combinations. A regular theme that crops up is many mums like to think of their daughter as their best friend. But if given an option to speak without giving offence (e.g. in the neutral space of the therapy room), the daughters often express unhappiness and even anger at that situation. However old the daughter may be – from 16 to 46 – what Jennie has found is that they want a boundaried mother–daughter relationship.

What this means in practice is the daughter may want to talk to their mum about all their difficulties, including their love life, but don't actually want to hear about Mum's love life or any similar emotional outpourings. Closeness doesn't equal transparency for this relationship to be healthy.

Mum might want to address who is in her friendship group and why she isn't getting her needs met from there. No child wants to be a confidante to their parent's relationships.

Friends filling a gap

As with a mum looking to her daughter to fill that close friend gap, we can also find ourselves looking for friends to fill a gap in our family – so this might be someone making friends with an older man as a father figure or an older woman as a mother or grandmother figure.

This is not necessarily wrong; it can be a very fulfilling relationship for both. What we need to be aware of is that we may subliminally make friends with someone who ends up not only filling that parent gap, but actually being the mirror image of the parent (which may not have been a healthy relationship).

Conclusion

Congratulations! You have now reached the end of the third Step of the book, tackling the emotionally delicate area of love and intimacy. This will have given you more insight into how you manage close alliances and prepared you for the relationships which many find most challenging – those inside the family unit.

Before you go on, reflect on what you have learnt about yourself in relation to love and friendship. In analysing your current or most recent relationship, what has surprised or pleased you most? What do you think needs changing – and are you ready to take the first step towards that goal? The following points may help, but don't be afraid to go back to Step One: Me, Myself, I if you need help with the concept of self-boundaries again.

Step Three Summary:
- A self-boundary is knowing how much to give to another while maintaining care for yourself.
- Draw a clear line between your past and current relationship.
- There's no rush to get a relationship on a better footing; pace, space and time will aid the process.
- Respect your partner and show it. From saying thank you and meaning it, to not shaming them in front of other people.
- Don't be too quick to paint yourself – or allow others to do so – as a villain. You may have been the hero of your story.
- Don't look elsewhere for something missing in you.
- Friends leave you feeling good (if sometimes rightfully challenged); a night out with a frenemy can drain you of energy and leave you feeling down.
- No child wants to be a confidante to a parent's relationships.

STEP FOUR:
YOUR FAMILY AND
OTHER ANIMALS

'Family not only need to consist of merely those whom we share blood, but also for those whom we'd give blood.'

CHARLES DICKENS

Our common fantasy family life draws on inspiration from those loving, yet chaotic groups in fiction like *The Waltons*, *Modern Family*, or even *The Munsters*. Who doesn't hark occasionally back to life in *Happy Days?* Reality is rarely that simple though.

In Step Four, we are going to look at family members in four sections: Parents/Elders; Children; Adolescents; and Siblings and Blended Families. You may find it helpful to start with the Parents section, even if your most obvious point of conflict is with a child or brother, as many of our patterns begin with 'Mum' and 'Dad'.

A family group needs boundaries just like the relationships we create through work or romance. But families come with some relationships ready-made – i.e. the one between your parents, that between siblings, etc. And they come with attitudes that have an impact which may be beyond anyone's control. Plus, the stakes can be higher, thanks to cultural pressures.

The trouble with this fantasy idea – the dream of the perfect family as a necessary goal for everyone – is that it affects your ability to build the very boundaries which could make it more real. Our need for a fantasy family weakens our ability to create a real one.

And it can feel artificial to control your boundaries with your family rather than letting them evolve 'naturally', but healthy boundaries will take you much closer to your dream of a happy family than relying on past behaviour or hoping for the best.

Families are not natural organisms that will automatically develop into the best shape for all participants. The family as we know it is very much an artificial construct based around tradition, fiction and masses of hope. So, at any point be aware that your biology does not *need* you to be in a family unit. It is just as 'natural' to be independent from some or all of your family as it is to be that nuclear image of the Modern Family, where everyone gets along somehow and meets for lunch on high days and holidays.

What we will do in this step is explore how boundaries can improve relationships between family members – whether you choose to stay in a large Waltons-type community, a 2+2, prefer a more solitary experience with occasional Christmas cards and FB postings, or complete self-sequestration. Understand that it is OK to live any way and boundaries will help you achieve this.

Let's stop and think how difficult this will be. We know boundaries in families may be the most awkward to tackle; that's why we've left them until you've had a bit of practice on yourself and less established relationships first.

Hopefully you will be more boundary-fit, having learnt a few skills and developed them in a more neutral setting. Take a moment to think of an occasion when you have used a boundary (or even just thought of one) since you began reading this book. Make a note of it in your Learning Journal.

Note that you are still reading this book. Well done on having a clear desire to address your boundaries, even if that desire is a very quiet or indeterminate voice at present. We're not expecting all readers to be boundary-ready at once; you may not even see the full benefit for some months after you put this book down.

Parents/Elders

What we all aim for is to deliver as parents – or to receive as children – is a 'good enough' experience.

Why just 'good enough'? Let's all mentally pick up a picture of the most famous happy family we can think of – whether that is the Dunphys in *Modern Family*, the Brockmans in *Outnumbered*, or the Ingalls family in *Little House on the Prairie*. Now rip that picture up. No family is perfect; let's take off the pressure. From this moment on, there is nothing to live up to; you decide the family you want to be part of.

> **Draw the Line:** *ditch your preconceptions about what should be: let's enjoy what is and what can be. That's what we mean by 'good enough'.*

This process will highlight what isn't good enough for you and your family and what can be done about that. Let's go forward from here.

EXERCISE: Draw Up Your Family

We're going to divide parents/elders (which includes grandparents, adoptive or foster parents, or any significant older person who played that type of role in your life) into three broad categories:

- Mr and Mrs Pedestal,
- Mr and Mrs Nightmare ('Oversteppers' and 'Ghosts'),
- Mr and Mrs Not-Bad.

(We've kept the 'Mr & Mrs' convention – simply because the stereotype emphasises the preposterousness of the idealised family.)

Create two or more lists in your Learning Journal – on one, write Parent 1, on the other, Parent 2. You can also add Parent 3, 4, or more to represent a step-parent/grandparent/carer as appropriate to your family set-up.

For each person, write down the answer to the following questions:

- What do I call this parent? (E.g. Mum, Daddy, Gramps, Mr Smith.)
- Are they alive?
- If so, do I know them? How well on a scale of 1–10? (1 = who they are by name only; 5 = polite conversation once a week, you know you can talk to them about their garden; 10 = I can always tell them how I am feeling.)
- Do they tell me they love me and do I reciprocate?
- Do I feel loved – when I'm with them and when I'm away?
- Can I talk to them about money (or other practical) difficulties?
- When I'm with them, do I feel child-like, either with a desire to be good and pleasing, or rebelling against all that they say and winding them up?
- Do I disagree with them (and is it OK to do that)?

- Am I aware of displeasing them; either now as a grown up or historically as a child?
- Do I ever wish they or I were someone else? This might be a real person, someone from fiction, or a fantasy construct bringing together longed-for characteristics found in a variety of people.

Now, examine your lists. From your answers, you will be creating a picture of how attentive your parents were towards you, how much you resented or enjoyed their level of attention and how well you feel you truly know each other.

Now consider if they match up (and to what degree) to the categories below.

Meet the Pedestal Parents

Mr and Mrs Pedestal might look like perfect parents. Perhaps you live close by, share weekly meals, support and enjoy each other's company, and hopefully feel loved and can love back in return. So, how can boundaries help you? Do you even need to adjust this relationship?

Perhaps. Do you truly view your relationship with them as equal or do you have them on a pedestal: 'they were the best parents/parent I could ever have', 'they are cleverer than me', 'better at juggling than me', 'better-looking than me', 'slimmer', 'taller than me'? As you consider those questions, visualise a pedestal and your parent/s on it – how high is it? What might that truly mean for you?

How does it feel to not feel good enough all the time, compared to their brilliance?

Traditionally this can be a problem for men – sons whose father had a glittering military or business career; women, though, will be catching up with this one in career terms as they achieve parity across the professions. Maybe your mother was a well-respected head teacher, or the first woman to campaign for this or that successfully. Maybe she was a perfect home-maker and mother. Either way, your idolisation of this type of parent doesn't allow much room for your own self-confidence.

To get them off their pedestal, it's not about demolishing them but building yourself up.

CASE HISTORY

John's father had been an extremely senior officer in the Armed Forces; John had decided at 10 he wanted to follow in Dad's footsteps. In therapy with Jennie, he recalled a childhood of his father returning from postings to exotic destinations, bearing presents, wearing smart uniforms – the excitement of coming home ceremonies and his mother beside herself with happiness and pride. It's not surprising that the little boy takes the decision and is applauded for doing so by both parents, for whom the military has been a rewarding and happy life.

What begins to diminish is the fledgling artist within John, who must be suppressed in order to bolster the young soldier. Fast forward 40 years and John has left the military and is running a big business near to where his parents have retired. He is disappointed with himself for having left the military and never achieving the public plaudits of his father's career, such as medals and honours.

To the outside world, this is a man who appears to have been successful in his military career, business and marriage; John himself would say he has done well. But never as well as his father. 'No one can beat the old man, he's a legend.'

It may be a surprise to know that this character would come for therapy and indeed this is someone who has been encouraged into it rather than actively sought it, due to his marriage beginning to break down.

John found it easier to blame an unhappy marriage for his present feelings rather than face what he would like from life, because that had been forgotten long ago. John's therapeutic journey was one of going back to his young self and remembering how he enjoyed creativity and how that whole side of him has been boxed up. By beginning to allow himself to access that creative box and understanding who that person may have been – rather than being the good boy following his father – he realised his unhappiness was not about his marriage, but derived from who he hadn't been.

Through learning about boundaries, John realised that the boundary with his father had not been healthy. This had enabled a boundary to be unconsciously imposed on him enforcing his career choice, rather than letting him find out what he would like to do.

For someone like John, it can take a long time to lower that pedestal. And for John to feel OK about making his own decisions about who he wants to be. Within his own boundary of who he wants to be, he can feel OK and he can see his father as OK – they don't have to be the same person.

This example shows that you don't have to be caught in a negative spiral with a pedestal parent (where you obviously resent their unmatchable success) to be affected by it. The damage can be quite subtle from an overwhelming, albeit loving, parent.

If John's father was open to the idea of boundary change too, he could – even now – emphasise the differences between them and show interest and pride in what John achieves in areas which are remote to his own successes.

Pedestal Parents #2 – 'Forever Parents'

Some of you will recognise Forever Parents – these are like Pedestal Parents but not as successful and perfect. They wouldn't expect you to follow their career; indeed, they make it clear you are welcome to stay at home until you decide what you want to do with your life.

Mum still does the washing and cooking, and Dad will sort out the car if it needs servicing or to drive you to work or collect you after a night out. Older readers may have gone back home after a divorce to discover they can pick up where they left off. What could possibly be wrong with having parents like that? No wonder you admire them: 'They are so kind; they do everything for me; it keeps them happy and feeling loved.'

Forever kids include the 30-something starting a new job and getting dropped by her father at the office. Or the young man who can't even make his new girlfriend a cup of tea. A newly-wed who has to call her mother for advice on using a washing machine or how to make up after a row.

Would you respect someone with such inadequate life skills? Would you want a relationship with them or to hire them? If asked the age of this character, what age would you put them at? Chances are it won't be 30.

If you accept that while life is smooth, you've not yet grown up (and may be the butt of some jokes among your peers). So, what are you getting out of this relationship?

You might believe you are inadequate or lazy, but the reality is you are unskilled in being a grown up and that can change.

We're not saying here that it is wrong to love or respect a parent, or for a parent to want to care for their child. But you are not a child anymore and it is time to shift that relationship to an adult ground for both of you.

BRING IN THE BOUNDARIES:

Your Pedestal Parents Plan

Pedestal Parents: Draw up a list of ways you differ from your parents – things you like about yourself, or things that you are good at that they are not. Find ways of being the person you wanted to be – whether it is the artist or the gardener. You need to set the boundary with yourself to validate and access that part of you without outside influence.

Forever Parents: Draw up a list of skills you need to learn – whether it is using a kettle or understanding your bank account. Knowledge is power, but it also supplies confidence. Build up a boundary: politely decline parental help whenever you can realistically do something yourself: 'Thank you, but I think that it is time I did that myself, don't you?' You might worry that your parents will be sad; you might also be disappointed if they are not. But you might also find a different way of being connected to them grows as a result.

Meet Mr and Mrs 'Nightmare' …

Within this description there are also two types: Oversteppers and Ghosts.

Oversteppers invade their child's boundaries (and that can be on a scale from physical/sexual abuse and neglect to enforced opinion on every part of the child's life, such as friendships, careers and who to vote for). These are the parents who have no compunction in reading a child's private diary. Or equally might discuss an adolescent's sexuality in front of them and others.

Ghosts are so uninterested in their child that they are simply not present either physically, emotionally, intellectually, or spiritually. At the extreme end, they are just a distant mark or memory on the horizon. Ghosts operate to different degrees – for some parents it may mean children sent to boarding school from the age of seven, to simply showing no interest in their school work.

Oversteppers

When Jennie visualises what we describe as Oversteppers, she sees giants in the child's life; invading every detail. You could also imagine bacteria spreading into every cell of you. Think of your skin boundary and how this type of parent seeps through effortlessly, however hard you try to maintain a firm response.

When children are small, they may not fully realise that this is not healthy parenting. At some level this may be displayed in physical signs of anxiety such as bedwetting, persistent nightmares, or playing running away games. For the child, the penny may not fully drop until they begin to interact with other people's families – and see how their friends are allowed to be themselves. This might include choosing what activities they want to do, voicing opinions without fear, being allowed to be vegetarian or not, being relaxed and noting the difference in the home.

Adolescence may be particularly volatile in an Overstepper home, thanks to the invigorating effect of hormones. A son who has always been physically punished may suddenly fight back. A daughter might run away for real. This is the time when you first begin to feel separate and different, naturally yearning towards more independence and developing your own opinions. But that inevitably leads to more clashes as the Oversteppers resent being challenged.

Adults with Overstepper parents don't leave behind the effects of this childhood when they do leave home (*if* they leave home, as this type of parenting can also result in the classic mother–daughter household, where a child feels honour-bound to stay at home and never leave, turning from child to carer).

If not turning into the carer, these young adults leave home as soon as they can – maybe by spending more and more time sleeping at a friend's house, going to university as far away as possible, or even leaving the country.

But unless they realise what is propelling them away, they may not be able to resist being pulled back into the controlled situation they grew up in and, returning to the Overstepper parents, reverting to whatever childhood behaviour has developed as a result of their upbringing.

So, for example, a child of Overstepper parents may find the only way to live in harmony at home is to submit to all requests and become child-like again, however old they get. Think of Norman Bates still trying to please Mother in *Psycho*'s Bates Motel.

And remaining a child will have an impact on their ability to have adult relationships with others and thus repeatedly ties them closer to home. In this scenario, any type of counselling or therapy is frowned upon by the parents, maybe even instinctively.

Some Oversteppers may feel like this because their own behaviour is due to their parents and, in these situations, there may be a cultural objection to seeking help outside the family unit, or even talking about 'things'. For the child of Oversteppers, a societal pressure of obedience and respect towards elders (especially parents) however they behave may be dominant.

Draw the Line: *there is no rule that says we must have a relationship with any other person – regardless of their biological or societal place in our lives. No one can force you to have any kind of*

*relationship – good or bad – with anyone else. You are your own
person and have a right to make your own decisions as to who is
in your life.*

'Chance makes our parents, but Choice makes our friends.'

JACQUES DELILLE

Shades of Overstepping

From the first inklings that your parents/carers are different to
the elders or parents in your friends' lives (which may happen
from about senior school age onwards as you spend longer at
other people's homes or go on holiday with another family) to
full realisation that you have giants in your life, you may recognise
that you've been overshadowed through all of your life, or simply
live in and out of the shade cast by them. Or they may cross your
boundaries only in certain aspects of your life.

For example, they may dominate your physical state: controlling
your access to medicines, or determining whether it is OK to be
poorly. They may dominate your career: deciding what you will do
and filling in forms for you, or offering financial support if you take
their chosen course at university. They may choose your politics for
you, demand you follow – or not – a religion, dictate your diet and
decide on your friends and, later, more intimate relationships. Or
all of the above, because some Oversteppers may stick to one area
of interference, but some will behave like this concerning every
aspect of their child's life.

As we get older, we get a clearer idea of what is right or wrong,
but when we are young we don't have that vision; even in cases
of sexual abuse a child will often not understand that a boundary
has been crossed.

EXERCISE: The Interference Spectrum

In your Learning Journal, draw a rainbow, with each colour band representing a different area in your life:

- Health
- Intimacy (non-sexual physical closeness and sharing of feelings)
- Career
- Finance
- Friends
- Lovers
- Values (politics, religion, etc.)

Now, using a black pen, shade in each layer where you feel your parents have Overstepped.

Be aware that not all shades need have the same density – you may feel your parents were domineering when it came to your friendships but only mildly interfering – though still effectually – in your religious ideas. This will give you an idea of how pervasive they were/are in your life.

Now, looking at the spectrum, consider what interference matters most to you. Is it all or just one section you want to deal with (at least initially)?

So, you might be comfortable with some level of dominance around your career – perhaps your parent is more of a Pedestal than a Nightmare – but their attitude towards your sexuality is negative and hostile and causing you pain.

CASE HISTORY

Jemma has grown up aware that her mother likes to look good and wants her to do so too. This means constant calorie counting, weighing and discussions about how Jemma looks.

In therapy with Jennie, Jemma joked about how her mother put her on a diet before her wedding, and chose and bought the dress, turning up with it on Jemma's doorstep unexpectedly. Jemma then laughed but with a grimace admitted that she did indeed wear that dress. But she felt it didn't matter as she knew her mother would outshine her on the wedding day anyway.

She laughs, but Jennie notices Jemma's eyes aren't laughing. Jemma says in passing that she doesn't have any photos of her wedding day up in her house.

Even after marriage and Jemma becoming a mum too – to a girl – the endless input on looks hasn't ended. Jemma was reprimanded over putting on too many pounds during pregnancy and warned to lose them swiftly, even before she took the baby home. Her mother will happily walk up to Jemma in public, point to her waistline and say, 'You really should cut back a bit, dear.'

The impetus to see Jennie came when Jemma noticed her own daughter – at 12 – begin to skip meals. She registered feeling uncomfortable when she overheard Granny warning her daughter about the danger of eating pudding. She also felt prickly when Granny admired her daughter for looking 'trim'. The discomfort grew when she found her daughter weighing herself on Jemma's scales.

Through conversation with Jennie, Jemma realised the effect of her mother on herself and her daughter, and her own potential influence on her daughter in future.

She realised she too was modelling the importance of looking good and had talked about her weight in front of her daughter, skipped meals and had been seen regularly weighing herself. Jemma was amazed by the knowledge that she too had been the conduit for the negative messages around food and looks which had dominated her own life.

She was aware that her mother was not dominating regarding other areas of her life, but this had been an unhealthy seam running throughout it so far. Cutting off all contact could be an overreaction but Jemma needed to do something as she didn't want to perpetuate the problem with her own daughter.

Jennie suggested that Jemma could start by looking to herself first – and her own self-boundaries. Even if she did not fully believe it, if she started talking in a positive way about herself not her body, this would have a positive effect not only for herself but also for her daughter.

Even if it doesn't feel right, this is brain re-training.

BRING IN THE BOUNDARIES:

Your Overstepper Plan

First, let us reassure you: *you are not alone.* You are not the first nor will you be the last person to realise you have/had giants in your life and to be perhaps a little scared of what this new knowledge means. You may not even want to read on and see our suggestions of how to help yourself deal with this reality, through boundaries.

To handle an Overstepper parent's demands you must build your self-confidence. One way of doing this is using daily affirmations. Science backs up the power of positive affirmation.

Let's use Jemma and her weight concerns as an example of how this will work. You could re-word these affirmations to suit the area you are concerned about.

Possible affirmations might be:

'*There's more to life than how I look.*'

'*I like the way I look.*'

'*I'm proud of how strong my body is.*'

'*I can make my own decision about what I look good in.*'

'*There's more to me than a waistline.*'

Step One: If, like Jemma, the word 'diet' has dominated your life, you can retrain your brain by taking that negative word and using it as a mental cue or mental jog to recite one of the positive affirmations listed above.

Step Two: Ditch the scales; just do it.

Step Three: Talk positively about looks in front of anyone over whom you may have an influence; make positive comments around areas such as emotional intelligence, kindness and academic ability – not just about looks.

Step Four: Tackle Mother. You might not need to have a head-on conversation about this with your Overstepping parent; through being positive about looks in general, changing the subject every time diet is talked about and meeting criticism with humour, a change will begin to take place.

Draw the Line: *if this is a persistent problem between a grandparent and a child, it is your duty as a parent to tell them to stop. You may* *not have been able to protect yourself as a child, but you do have a duty to protect your child.*

Remembering the Drama Triangle, the mother might become more Persecutory and increase her criticism, and that is the point to talk directly to her.

In Jemma's case, this meant owning her words: for example, saying something like, 'I have been thinking about my attitude to food and how I look, and realised I'm not happy with it.'

'I have also realised that it is having a knock-on effect on my daughter.

'I'm working at changing it around for my sake and for my daughter's sake. And I would appreciate your support in doing this.

'I'm asking if we can change conversations around food and looks, and preferably find other things to talk about.'

Jemma decided to end it with a question – employing her mother's thinking, not her feeling – and asking, 'What do you think about that?'

Draw the Line: *remember, to keep 'boundaried' you are not defending a dissertation (giving reasons and examples); it's enough to state what you want.*

Some readers will be feeling a little 'itchy' at this conversation, thinking: 'I couldn't say that', 'I wouldn't be listened to', 'It wouldn't have any effect', or even 'It might make things worse'.

Remember, overstepping occurs across a spectrum. Some will find their Overstepping parents easier to deal with than others, possibly depending on the subject. But fear is no reason not to start somewhere and, if this is an opening gambit in a much longer sequence of events, it's still a realistic place to start.

Take heart: even a tiny reinforcement of a small boundary can start you on a process towards feeling better about yourself and stronger and healthier overall.

The Ghosts

These are the parents without substance. If your parents are deceased their influence may be so strong it seems to keep them with you like a 'ghost', but for some children, the parents are never truly there even when alive. They are shadows whispering through your life.

Ghosts are lost to you either physically or emotionally; in character, they may appear friendly or firm, but the relationship is characterised with an underlying indifference. But like the Overstepping relationship, Ghosts are on a spectrum, with some showing interest in a few areas of their children's lives, and others showing no interest whatsoever.

CASE HISTORY

Eleanor is a corporate lawyer and single mother who came to see Jennie about her relationship with her 15-year-old daughter, Louise, who had become distant. She told Jennie that she had been a reliable parent, always on hand to discuss academic matters, and had taken time off work to attend parent-teacher meetings and school awards nights. She always made space for discussing projects and exam choices. But that left few moments for discussing Louise's friendships, budding romances, sports events, or even her diet, clothes and health.

She says that she has even asked Louise if she is a good parent and her daughter always says yes and that she is proud of her mother's career, but has sometimes seemed a little sad that there was no time for hanging out.

Talking to Jennie, Eleanor began to realise that she was a Ghost parent, defending that by explaining that her interest in Louise's school results was more important than spending a Saturday shopping for clothes together. She said: 'I have done my best'.

This is not an uncommon stereotype in modern society – and it is understandable. The hard-working single parent must make tough choices where time is concerned and will not always get them right. Eleanor may justify to herself that she spent time on the most important element in Louise's life (her professional future), but Louise has other emotional needs which are not being met.

It's worth noting that a parent like Eleanor – most probably a by-product of her own upbringing – is also not getting her full needs met as she is denying herself the pleasure of a close emotional bond with her child.

In some families, there is a Ghost parent and a functioning parent. This may be because there has been bereavement or divorce, or simply that the Ghost is present physically, but not emotionally.

Typically, if we are working outside the home, we have periods of being absent from our children. What we're talking about here is a parent that is not 'available' even when they are with their children. (Once again technology plays a part in this – if we wanted to, we could all be working 24 hours a day, checking e-mails and sending messages.)

Draw the Line: *technology has blurred our work boundaries and this is having a negative effect on our children.*

Not all Ghost relationships are as inherently well meaning. Some children grow up with parents who are Ghostly in every area. These might be the Loved-Up Couple, who are still so into each other, they can't spare emotion for their children. They might be the Work Abroad couple, where one partner takes a job overseas and their husband/wife decides to join them, sending children off to boarding school. The Taxi couple fit in here too – these parents might live in the same country and send their children to local schools, but project manage their time so intensively with after-school clubs, full weekend activities and constant sleepovers. This could be for whatever reason (including the children's apparent skill development, or their own social life or social status). In doing so, they are bypassing the most important part of a child's emotional development – the connection to their parent.

Then there is the Mix–Match Pair – where the couple is in a strong Parent–Child dynamic, which can lead to one parent turning into a Ghost when children come along. If a parent spends a lot of their time in a Child-like position, they won't be available to their children.

And lastly, there are the Victorian Parents – the ones who simply believe it is wrong to be too close to one's children, living in an arcane and distant fashion.

There are times when the children of Ghosts will be envied by their peers – they might be allowed to do what they want, there won't be all that fussing. There will be few – or no – boundaries. The child may feel quite cool. And they may find comfort elsewhere.

Joe Strummer of The Clash has said: 'The only place I considered home was the boarding school, in Yorkshire, my parents sent me to.'

Children of Ghosts often perpetuate this model as they simply have no idea how to parent, having not seen it.

BRING IN THE BOUNDARIES:

Your Ghost Parent Plan

Obviously, solutions will differ depending on how intensely absent your parent is or was. Cognitively, you most probably say to yourself and others it was OK. You may have lots of friends who have had similar circumstances.

So, we're not suggesting that you go on a Ghost hunt to bring back those lost parents. One of the hardest lessons of adolescence is that you cannot make someone else love you or want to spend time with you, no matter what you do or offer. So instead, how do we deal with the impact of Ghost parents on ourselves? First, it requires an honest internal dialogue. You might be thinking: 'I'm fine. I'm OK. School was OK. I've got loads of friends. I don't see a problem.'

But what might have been said to you over the years from partners you have batted away? Might it be comments such as: 'I never know what is going on with you', 'you're very independent', 'you don't need me', 'I don't know what you're feeling', 'you're cold', 'you take everything as a joke', 'you like your friends more than you like me', or 'you're self-reliant'?

Think about how these comments made you feel. Can you admit to yourself you struggle to be close to another? Is it difficult to maintain a long-term relationship?

Now, we'd like you to write down in your Learning Journal a description of your ideal parent – they could be imaginary, a character from a book or a real person – either famous or familiar (e.g. a friend's parents). You can draw them in your Learning Journal or cut a photo out and stick it in. Now make a note of the qualities they possess which you so admire. Perhaps they are loving or strict, exciting or calming?

Looking at those attributes, how many of them do you apply to yourself? Do you give yourself enough praise or love? Are you caring towards yourself? Could you be that better parent to yourself?

Make a sentence you could say to yourself each day that would sound as if it came from a truly present parent, such as: 'I'm glad you are in my life,' or 'You are worth my time and attention'.

Are you turning into a Ghost too?

Look at yourself again: would you say you are able to form deep, honest and trusting relationships that are mutually satis-fying – or do you find it easier (even if not preferable) to be on your own? If you want to come back from the other side, what can you do?

If you are really honest and visualise your self-boundary now, what does it look like? Don't be surprised if it looks like a high wall or other insurmountable obstacle.

Draw the Line: *when we get used to living without nurture as children, it's hard to nurture ourselves. From today, start thinking of ways to be kinder to yourself.*

Ultimately, surviving a Ghostly upbringing is about taking the risk of letting another care for you and look after you and see your vulnerability. In doing that, the long-neglected child inside you will heave a sigh of relief.

Combination parents

You may have recognised elements of both Nightmare and Pedestal Parents in your own mother and father. Perhaps your dad was a Ghost – absent on business, but hugely successful so you find it easier to place him on a pedestal than to be angry at his lack of interest in you.

Or sometimes the Ghost parent helps elevate the present parent to a pedestal – it is hard to see any fault (and there is a fear of any fault) in the remaining parent. In the child's eye they have to be perfect to make up for the absent other.

Another pairing might be a Ghost with an Overstepper. The latter parent is so dominant that the former becomes a Ghost and hands over all decision-making and responsibility. To the actual child, they may feel absent or even like a sibling.

This could look like a very controlling father who never really wanted offspring with a child-like mother who thinks they would be fun and so therefore gets pregnant. While the child is very young this mother can respond to the baby's needs as she likes playing being Mummy with a dolly; once the child becomes older and has greater needs, emotionally and physically, the mother begins to withdraw as it puts her in the position of having to grow up and not be playing Mummy anymore. The mother may also place more importance on keeping the father who never wanted children happy so concentrates more on that relationship, keeping their own Parent-Child dynamic going and thus becomes more of a sibling to her own baby.

Note that a Ghost parent can force the other parent into an Overstepper role: 'someone has to be in charge, I'll show them how to do this'. And conversely, an Overstepper can create a Ghost: 'I don't need your help with anything, you're no good at hands-on parenting anyway. I need you to work really hard so I can enjoy being a supported stay-at-home parent'.

Take a moment to consider your favourite fairytales. Traditionally, the stories begin with at least one absent parent. The mother may die, the father may be away on a quest and the children must prove their independence and ability to survive without supportive parents.

Whatever the set of circumstances, not having the parent/s means there is a lack of a healthy boundary – either it is being invaded by the Oversteppers or there is no boundary at all where Ghosts exist. You can't negotiate a boundary with a Ghost or an Overstepper, you must fix your own and stay firm.

Meet The Not-Bads ...

If you have the Not-Bads as parents, you are not too far away from the more ideal Good Enoughs.

Not-Bads are the parental figures who are over-controlling in some instances and uninterested in other circumstances, perhaps too judgemental sometimes or unable to resist invading your space, or simply stand back too far from your space. So, if you recognise these parents, then you may wonder 'what can I do?' After all, sometimes they can be a nightmare, but other times you seem to rub along OK. Why change and risk upsetting the status quo, which is only frustrating some of the time?

Draw the Line: *all relationships have to be worked on. Just because you have been in a relationship for a long time doesn't mean it doesn't need attention.*

BRING IN THE BOUNDARIES:

Your Not-Bad Parent Plan

The first thing to establish is, do you want more or less from your parents? Now think about how you can make that happen.

If the majority of contact you have with the parent is helping you out – e.g. dog walking or school run – how about looking at how you can have contact with them through it not being a helping role? Asking them round just for a cup of coffee, for example. Or why not join them in an activity or gentle hobby as equals – like gardening, or walking around a National Trust house together, or going shopping.

If your parents are Not-Bads, remember your relationship will be full of ups and downs, so bear in mind that boundaries have those flexible walls. Ease your way into a more comfortable relationship. Don't fall into the trap of 'that's just the way it is, that is the way they are' – remember every relationship can be improved and you can be a decisive part of that.

EXERCISE: Space Rocket*

Imagine there is a space rocket docked outside your house. You have 24 hours to decide who is going in that space rocket with you. There is no limit either way.

It is going to go to a new planet with everything on it that you like about this planet – think job, house and country. But it is a one-way journey. You decide who goes on that space rocket and you don't have to give any reason or explain yourself as to why. Write down

---

* Listen to this visualisation exercise for free on Soundcloud at bit.ly/space-rocket

the names below. Some may be a surprise. It is important to listen to your heart and not do what you feel you 'should' do. If someone feels scary, don't ignore that feeling.

Remember, this list is for your eyes only.

Those who are on your rocket are the ones that you need to concentrate on here on planet Earth.

You may notice that the ones you wanted to leave behind are those that you seem to spend a lot of your time thinking and worrying about. They are also the least likely to support your needs in return.

It's time to redress the balance.

Are you feeling uncomfortable with this exercise? Perhaps you are worried about the feelings of those who you are choosing to leave behind, worried about their reaction? (Try this exercise again but imagining that no one is offended or hurt by their non-selection.) This could be a wake-up call for you to how much of a Rescuer you are. Perhaps concentrate instead on the people you do want to be with; is your relationship with them more balanced?

Another note of warning: what if your rocket is empty? Is this illustrative of your need to widen your social circle and seek out new relationships?

People in healthy relationships 'feed' each other with equal amounts of support, nurture and stimulation. If you feel like you are always the feeder and never the fed, is it time to reappraise?

When you are the parent

Looking at our own mothers and fathers, we can see that it's surprisingly easy to be a Not Good–Enough Parent. Happily, getting to the position where you are Good Enough is not complicated or difficult. It will require setting healthy boundaries for yourself, but also for your child.

And the first boundary of being a parent is with yourself. Sifting or sorting through some of your parents' values and beliefs you hold – deciding which ones you want to hold on to or were helpful and those which were never helpful and need to be ditched.

Moreover, if there are two of you parenting this is a discussion to be had between both parties and preferably before the child comes along. We'll address this in the next section.

Children

Let's consider again why a child needs boundaries.

Think about a child learning to walk and the thrill they experience when they start taking their first few steps. Some children will want to hold on to something or someone – but some don't. Some just want to go as fast as they can. Especially if they have older siblings and are trying to catch up. But it is a very natural response to keep them safe. To hold their hand. To give them a push-along toy for support, to give them a cheer when they make progress, but also a cuddle when they go too far and get hurt.

This could be used as a metaphor for boundaries throughout a child's life, with you the 'Good Enough' parent supporting and encouraging, holding their hand when they need it, but letting them have a go on their own when they are ready.

Overall, giving a child clear boundaries can be seen as active parenting, a way to support and encourage development within a realistic and thoughtful framework which neither inhibits nor suppresses, nor exposes to danger. Boundaries for children might have a slightly negative connotation but it is not all about saying 'no' or tapping into your Victorian self. Boundaries can support a child towards freedom and independence.

Many parents may be reading this book in snatches, taken perhaps when a first child is asleep. So we've chosen to divide this section into practical topics that can be worked through individually. You might like to look at the early steps again if you need to get your bearings and reinforce your own boundaries before you tackle those of your offspring.

Night Night, Sleep Tight

There is much advice and many books already which will tell you how to get your baby either into a routine, or following the attachment model where sleep, like eating, is baby-led. The most important advice from us on this point is to follow and trust your instincts and do what works for you and your family.

But at some point, when a child is naturally beginning to sleep through the night and/or has been moved to their own bed, and is out of the cot (which can physically contain or control a child), you will need to help them establish a boundary around bedtime. This sleep boundary is one that will be useful to them throughout life.

First, consider how much sleep your child needs. According to the NHS, a six-month-old baby needs three hours in the daytime and 11 hours at night. At two years, they require 90 minutes during the day and 11 and a half hours at night; by six, it's dropped to 10 hours and 45 minutes at night; and at nine a child needs 10 hours at night. Up to aged 16, nine hours is still recommended.

But your child doesn't know these numbers; they may be naturally good at listening to their body and comfortable in falling asleep. Or they may naturally be highly responsive to stimuli and eager to stay awake and enjoy it. Or you may be feeding their wakefulness by poor boundaries which allow them to watch TV late at night, play on computers or tablets, or eat something sweet before bedtime which will raise their blood sugar.

The boundary can be too 'tight' as well – think of the family who send children to bed super-early, with instructions not to disturb them. These children may simply not be ready to sleep and find their own ways to be amused, which will also keep them awake (even if the parents don't know).

Hold the boundary that you decide works for what your child needs and for you as a family. Think of the facts of how much sleep a child needs. Start there and decide how you are going to achieve that.

BRING IN THE BOUNDARIES:

Your Child Sleep Plan

1. There's enough proof now that blue screen stimulus is not advisable in the bedroom for any of us, so any computer/ tablet/phone/TV must live outside the bedroom. Establish a family area where everything stays at night (maybe a basket on the stairs).

2. Sleep-proof the room. Curtains should be lined with black-out fabric; check how much ambient noise your child is exposed to, particularly in the first hours when sleep is light. Could you go to sleep with the indistinct booming of a TV in a lower room? How can you expect your child to do differently?

3. Decide on a watershed. This is the time your child goes up to bed even if there is still time for stories, cuddles, or a bath. To help you choose this time, think of when your child has to get up and count backwards. Build in the hours you know

they need to sleep and see where that takes you for a starting point. For example, if your child doesn't have to get up till 8 a.m., and that suits them as well, your night-time boundary can be later than if they naturally wake at 6 a.m. (or have to for practical reasons).

4. Conscious cuddles. At the point your watershed starts, take a moment together to have a hug and pause. It can act as a physical symbol that the night boundary has begun.

5. Reading. An important part of the night boundary is a book. Whether it's a page or a chapter, your commitment to them is comforting when it comes through the prism of a good book shared. Save audio books and podcasts for car journeys, if possible, as they are usually being played on a device.

6. Overall point. You will know how long your routine will take – 15 minutes, 30 minutes, maybe an hour? But once you establish the boundary and you know how long it takes, stick to it. Don't get derailed – this is reality. Illness can stretch a boundary, as can a physical change like moving house. But remember, boundaries can stretch for short periods, before they need to be eased back into place. Stick to the length of time you need to get your child to bed.

As they get older, children may take the precise moment they know you are leaving the bedroom to unleash some emotional trauma experienced that day, but don't be put off by this. Remember, if this takes you out of your bedtime boundary this will not be beneficial to the child. So, acknowledge what they are saying, agree to talk about it in the morning and give them something else to think about such as their new Lego kit they have to build. Or suggest they imagine that they are playing some loved sport. Or ask them to think of some family member or pet who is warm and comforting. Keep it short. Say goodnight and turn the light out.

What to do if your child calls out or gets up? At the first call out, open their door, but don't go into the room, showing that this is meant to be sleep time. Ask what is wrong. Respond appropriately. It might be the curtains aren't shut properly and light is coming in. It could be they say they are thirsty – but are they really? If you think about it, you know they have had enough to drink during the day – if not, do give them a drink and make a mental note to check that earlier tomorrow night. Say kindly but firmly that it is now bedtime and stick to it.

> **Draw the Line:** *as children get older, you can appeal to their heads as well as their hearts and point out that prolonged delaying at bedtime means an earlier bedtime (five or ten minutes) the next night. Say it and mean it.*

What about night terrors?

Genuine distress shouldn't be ignored, but the time to deal with the underlying issues is during the day and in a focused way. In the night, there needs to be soothing and reassurance and to tell the child the problem will be dealt with.

Attack the root cause of distress and the symptoms will naturally ease, although this may take some time to diagnose and treat.

Morning!

Just like a night-time boundary – establish your daytime boundary that works for the whole family and stick with it. So that means getting up at the same time every day and following an agreed set of behaviour (washing, dressing, breakfasting) within that time frame. Bear in mind your teenager may not be exaggerating when they say they need to get up later than you. But that doesn't mean lying in bed all day either as they will end up with a disrupted body clock.

If coming from a place of no boundaries around bedtime this is going to take a while to establish – possibly months – be patient and stick with it. You will all benefit.

The joy of sleepovers?

There seems to be a growing trend for pre-teen sleepovers. Whether it's individual nights or parties, in the house or in tents, the pressure for young children to spend a night away from home before they are ready is immense. And that social pressure extends to their parents too. Sleepovers used to be a teenage treat, never during a school week and often for a maximum of three children.

Now, children as young as four and five are routinely sent off for sleepovers – on a school night too – and sometimes for a couple of nights in a row. This is not the same as staying with relatives where the house is familiar and the child's routine most probably adhered to and they are sleeping as normal, probably on their own.

The modern sleepover seems to involve no limits – in terms of bedtime, entertainment and sweet consumption. Is this part of a trend towards making our children grow up faster than ever before (while we loudly declaim the same thing on TV and in society generally)? We say it's a tragedy childhood is becoming more fleeting, but what's our part in it?

Why do we assume that sleepovers are either necessary or beneficial or fun for the child?

Of course, some parents – particularly those with only children – may be desperate to give them that sense of Famous Five-type fun which often comes as standard with a larger family. But family camping or a spontaneous midnight feast with your siblings is not the same as being herded off with strange children and told to have fun in a house you don't know, with rules you don't understand. And with adults you don't know or trust.

At the end of a perfectly pleasant supper party, do you want to go home to your own bed, or are you happy to sleep on the floor, find a strange bathroom in the dark, adhere to someone else's rules and not be 100 per cent sure when you could leave?

We can all get caught up in trends – and this is one. It's also an ideal chance to establish a clear boundary and stick with it. Decide for yourself and your family how you feel about sleepovers and what age you think your child is mature enough to really want to do this (not just to convenience you or please another family).

Draw the Line: *secondary school is quite old enough for sleepovers to start. Children of primary school age need to sleep in their own beds every night. For them, a party is pass the parcel, not the sleeping bag.*

Consider past times: in the Victorian era, children were expected to be much more independent at a young age, but as a society we have agreed that this is not desirable and that our youngsters should be given the chance to grow up and mature slowly, leaving them more confident and secure in adulthood.

Consider also nature: fledglings who are evicted from the nest too soon literally are not ready to fly. All animals, including humans, need time to mature; it will make them far more independent in the long run.

The same advice could go for school trips at primary level. How can it be OK for a child to be suddenly in a position where they are unable to contact their parents/caregiver for five days? There seems to be a British cultural trend for believing that not only do our children need to be able to cope alone from a young age, but also they are somehow inherently equipped to do so.

A parent may say, well, they came back OK, but there is a vast difference between surviving a situation and enjoying (and learning from) it. It's part of the normalisation of separation.

> **Draw the Line:** *building a strong family is like making a glossy roux sauce. Consistency is everything – both parents must follow the same recipe.*

The importance of the united boundary cannot be understated – and it's never too late to have that conversation with your partner.

If you are a single parent, you may be aware that being the only parent to decide on the family boundary is one of the advantages of your position. But couples do need to agree on where their joint boundary lies before it gets tested.

So this means even with a toddler, there is no crossing lines. If Mum says it's bedtime, Dad backs her up (even if he has only just got home and fancied an extra hour of family play). If you don't agree with the boundary being held, talk about it out of the child's earshot so any temporary adjustment still comes from the parents as one unit. Children will sense when there isn't a united boundary and will push to find the weaker link.

Food Glorious Food

Which brings us to food . . .

Mealtimes are minefields in many households, but they don't have to be.

First, think back to the section on self-boundaries where we asked you to look at your own attitude to food and 'healthy eating'. You are modelling a relationship with food for your child. So, from the mother on the perpetual diet to the dad who eats nothing but pizza and chips, be aware that the most influential driver on your child's eating habits is not the TV or advertisements or his friends or school: it's you. You can't expect them to be tucking into five portions a day if they never see broccoli passing your lips.

Again, there is enough dietary information already available so we're not going to offer nutritional guidelines here – you can access a Healthy Eating Fact Sheet from the British Dietetic Association online. However, there are areas around choice and pattern you can influence, as long as you bear in mind the boundary that we need to establish here.

This boundary is quite similar to sleep – we want to make sure our children get enough food, that it is generally the right sort of food and that they have a relationship with eating which is comfortable, neither fearing food nor becoming obsessed with it.

One of the underlying problems in establishing this boundary is that British children (and increasingly, other Western nations) are fed a separate diet from their parents. Broadly speaking, nursery food.

Could this be a result of our historic class system, especially in Victorian times, where it was traditional to keep 'higher class' children separate from parents, feeding them like exotic species on overly palatable food such as milk puddings? Poor children would of course be glad to eat whatever their parents ate and lack of money meant less choice/less food anyway.

Fast forward in our aspirational culture and this is one idea we all seem to have aped; with children still offered a 'palatable' range of food (portions, shapes, bland or sweet flavours) to encourage them to eat, when they are at an age when they would probably eat anything.

Certainly, parents in France would be surprised at how little in common British kids' meals have with their parents' meals, as French children are encouraged to eat what their parents eat at a much younger age.

This disparity means we set up children to expect different food – which is sweeter, blander and fussier in general – and then when aged about eight we declare that we want them to conform to 'healthy eating' as directed by society (e.g. ten a day), to their surprise and resentment. They feel like their palates have already been shaped and that 'adult' food is sourer, more bitter, more complex and chewy than they feel used to. And isn't shaped like a dinosaur.

So how do we break the cycle?

BRING IN THE BOUNDARIES:

Your Child's Eating Plan

Baby-led weaning is a start; rather than filling the freezer with endless liquidised vegetables, you can allow a baby from six months (as they start to show interest) to chew on whatever you are eating as long as it isn't high in sugar and salt. Already you are establishing a boundary that says, 'We all eat the same thing and we're going in the right direction.'

As children grow up, however, fussiness does become a common issue and some of that can be about the child wanting to push the boundary and/or wanting to assert their own taste.

The following suggestions will help:

a) Are separate meals the best use of your time?

Families who fall into the trap of making a variety of options at one mealtime are signaling some food isn't OK. A clear boundary around mealtimes means all the family have a version of the same meal, by which it might mean no salt in the children's portion or vegetarian meat substitute in half the cooking, but overall the family sit down together to the same menu.

The more options you offer a young child at each mealtime, the more you are confusing them. And you can't blame a child for being dazzled by choice or power. So as they grow you can begin to offer choice within the parameters of what you can realistically provide.

Example: If you have chicken fillets, an older child may be asked whether they want chicken curry or pasta bake. As we would ask our partner. Or sometimes we take the decision on what is going to be eaten. This means the boundary is growing like a belt with the child.

b) Sitting together

Getting everyone to the table for meals can feel like a nightmare, but it's still a vital part of family life. You can't expect to be sat around a table like the Waltons, saying grace and passing the sweetcorn, but there are certain meals where we can sit and eat at the same time, and this is respectful to the family unit. One parent may be involved so heavily in meal preparation (and solving all the tiny practical problems of a meal) they don't sit down at all. Another parent might be so used to eating quickly that they have finished before anyone has relaxed enough to talk. Note: children often get an instant energy burst from a meal, which can encourage them to talk and open up.

Draw the Line: *phones do not belong at a family meal table and actually neither do newspapers. Don't shut out your dining companions, however old they are.*

c) Table manners

We're never going to aspire to the *Downton Abbey* era of table manners, but there is no reason to throw the baby out with the bathwater. Encouraging children to hold their knife and fork correctly makes it easier for them to eat efficiently, will help avoid indigestion, prevents crockery being knocked to the floor or water being spilt and in the long run allows mealtimes to be a calm space where conversation can emerge.

d) Parental messages

We mentioned modelling at the beginning; take a minute to think about how you eat in front of your child or children. Do you provide them with a balanced meal, but they never see you eating a carb or a vegetable? What message are you giving them? You really can't expect them to eat a wide range of foodstuffs if you model the attitude that 'it is grown up to be fussy'.

Think about what portion size you consume – do you deny yourself seconds even if you are still hungry (or the meal is your favourite)? Or do you always leave certain foods off your plate?

Do you have a clinical reason why you can't eat certain foods – e.g. diagnosed Coeliac disease (allergy to the protein in wheat)? Or do you have a profound moral objection, say, to eating farmed chicken? These are positions which you need to explain to your children when they are old enough to understand. Remember, children notice everything, even if they don't comment.

e) Preparing and cooking food

Do you involve your child in this activity (regardless of gender)? There's little doubt that involving a child with food preparation will encourage them to eat new foods and teaches them where food comes from and how flavours are put together. This in turn can encourage them to eat more interesting foods. And thus supports the idea of a family who eat the same meal together.

Ring a Ring o' Roses – the family boundary

We've talked about sleepovers and eating; clearly, these are the type of boundaries you may set which are more vulnerable to being pushed by other parents, potentially causing conflict between you and your children. It's the classic scenario with teenagers, where they demand to behave in a certain way because that's what happens when they are with friends whose parents may not share your values.

Imagine the boundary around your child extending now to around you, a partner and your children, so that there is one set of agreed behaviours which you all adhere to whether you are together or not. Some of these may be straightforward – no one in your family steals, for example – some may inevitably change over time, such as political or religious beliefs. Some, though, could stay strong yet flexible consistently. Only you (and a partner) can decide which these might be, and you (and that partner) can create them.

The overanxious parent

For some, the parenting stakes feel higher. These may be the individuals or couples who have struggled to become parents, sometimes for years, or who may have lost a child. They may feel more intensely the need for perfection in the home and in perfect parenting at all costs. This can also be driven by superstition – how to stop the worst happening again; or being tied to feelings of inadequacy or being undeserving.

To solve this, parents need to spend time together outside the family home when they can talk without interruption – but not late at night. (This might involve booking some childcare.) Talk through how you are both experiencing life now and how that compares with what you dreamed of. Chances are it will be very different. Now project forward – how will the landscape look in two years' time if you keep striving for perfection in this way? Will you all be happier – or will it be worse?

Talk about what you individually need to change – how can you support each other and yourself in those changes? How can you get pleasure back in your life?

And might you have closed in as a family because of what you have been through and lost outside support? How can you take steps to allow the outside world back in? You don't need to be in control all the time to be safe. Take time to appreciate what you have, grieve for what you have lost but then allow yourself to carry on.

Sit with your partner or, if you are single, a trusted friend and talk about the source of your anxiety. Many women and men who have suffered recurrent miscarriages, for example, talk of being haunted by the unborn children in their lives. Addressing these children out loud can be helpful. Ideally find your own words but a variation of the following might be a starting place: 'I love you and will always hold you in my heart and now I need to let you go in peace.'

Computer Games and Social Media

What is your opinion on computer game playing and screen time? Has it changed since you started using this book, especially after reading the step on self-boundaries and the Internet? Take this moment to look back at your Learning Journal.

So now, think about how you feel about computer games and social media when your children are doing it. You might hold any of the following largely positive views: it's a great thing, keeps children up to date with the real world, is something I can do with my child, enhances mental flexibility and helps with necessary entertainment while I'm working or doing chores.

At the other end of the scale are parents who might believe that not only does game playing stifle creativity and imagination, it contributes to obesity through lack of exercise, isolates the child and costs them social skills experience, and is anti-social in general.

We are not being pejorative here; you must decide where you are on that scale – perhaps taking into account other factors such as where you live, or whether your child has to travel a lot, for example. And it's worth noting that according to experts, the time a child spends online and on social media may not be hours lost to additional homework, but the twenty-first century equivalent of hanging around the bus stop with friends drinking cider.

If possible, decide your boundaries before your child becomes aware of gaming so your ethos is in place because whatever your decision, as soon as they start school that boundary will be leant against.

We all know the cry of 'Everyone's doing it' from a child and the allure of advertising. But think ahead, because this first boundary might apply to technology, but that cry will soon recur about a lot of behaviour on which you may have strong opinions. The idea of defining your ground before it becomes an issue will help your family stay united and help your child – when away from the family unit – stay true to what they believe and know to be right rather than getting caught up in peer pressure.

So your first boundary may be around computers, but notice its effect. It's the same boundary muscle you will want to flex around friendships, staying out, eating, youthful relationships, ear piercing and tattoos, sleepovers and parties which contribute to so much family angst as children turn into young adults.

It's also worth thinking about what choices you are offering as an alternative to playing on a gadget or screen. Are you suggesting they get off the iPad and do some homework or household chores? Or are you offering to spend the time together making a cake, going for a bike ride, or playing an imaginary game?

Be honest: are the gadgets a useful babysitter, allowing you to get on with work or your own online hobby or amusement?

Needs v Treats

One way to decide where a boundary lies in these type of cases, is to consider Needs v Treats. For example, how do you feel about your young children having mobile phones? Do you think it is harmless fun, something everybody does, a chance to reward them for good behaviour, a special Christmas present, or a useful tool to help them stay in touch as they spend more time away from you at school or other activities?

This debate seems to rage particularly loud around the school Years 4 to 7 – so how can you find a solution that fits with your family boundary? Consider whether a phone would be a useful item (need) which would help your child in a practical sense and which they are mature enough to care for responsibly. Or is it a treat – something you have bought them to cheer them up or to fit in with their friends (ask here who is in charge of the boundary)? Or because you have become used to buying relatively extravagant or generous presents for Christmas or birthdays and you have run out of other options?

Good boundary-making considers needs and is flexible enough to accommodate them: 'You can have a phone but not till you start senior school'. Poor boundary-making results when you are too governed by the need to treat, reward, or influence behaviour. If your child's life is governed by their peers, where is the parenting in that?

Draw the Line: *if children learn that boundaries can be easily breached by outside influences, how safe will they feel when the bigger issues come along – say, sex? And who will redefine those boundaries when you are already parenting on the back foot?*

Saving face

Don't assume your child always enjoys a lack of boundaries, they may be more grateful than you know to have them clearly in place.

Think of a 16-year-old girl asked to a party where she knows there will be pressure placed on her to drink alcohol, smoke and maybe sleep with a boyfriend. She may appear cross if you as the parent remind her of the family boundaries which you expect her to keep to – not drinking or smoking, and indeed perhaps not even going if the event is not being supervised. However, she may simply not know how to say 'No' by herself and be relying on you to enforce a boundary that she does feel comfortable with, and which helps her save face in front of her peer group. Part of her may rile against you, the other half may be quite relieved.

EXERCISE: Needs v Treats

For the following demands applied to children under 16, which would you deem 'Need' or 'Treat', given your own family boundaries? Make a note in your Learning Journal. How many Needs v Treats does your child have? Are you surprised by the result?

- Mobile phone? N or T
- Games consoles? N or T
- Ear piercing? N or T
- Tattoo? N or T
- Sleepovers? N or T
- After-school clubs? N or T
- New trainers? N or T
- Own PC? N or T
- TV in the bedroom? N or T

Sharing the boundaries

When you set up these boundaries it may be before your children are in a position to have opinions of their own. But once they start to become more articulate and more interested in the world, it can be useful to have regular family meetings, where you not only explain what the family boundaries look like, but why they are in place and how they benefit everyone.

This means you need to model these boundaries too – it's no good complaining about your adolescent always being on their mobile if you are too, even when you justify it as essential work. No one has to be 'on' 24/7. Be aware of when children do approach you to talk; if you are on a computer, tablet, or phone, make a clear show of putting it down in order to give them your full attention. So this way, children can grow up understanding how to put their own boundaries in place if they need to when you are not around.

Adolescents

Modern British culture seems to fetishise the unhappy and troubled adolescence – it seems no child can avoid it, no parent can cope with it. There are even advocates who suggest a child must rebel in order to become a separate person; that if the apron cord is not cut violently, natural separation will not occur.

We take a different view. Adolescence does not have to be one long painful battleground. Indeed, if you view it as inevitable conflict, are you creating a self-fulfilling prophecy?

Instead, try viewing the landscape ahead differently. Think back to being a parent of a toddler on a picnic. You sit on the rug dishing out food, drinks, plasters, sunscreen, hats and cuddles when required. Initially the toddler stays very close, but as they gain confidence and become more curious they move further and further away from the rug, for longer and longer, returning to you only when they need something practical or want emotional reassurance.

Your job is to keep an eye on them. When they go out of sight, you might need to stand up and look for them. You might need to fetch them back. And point out how far they can go. You would certainly warn them of dangers such as open water or a road.

They may be playing very happily within your eyesight but then take fright at a sudden bee and rush back to your arms. They know you are there to reassure them and then they can venture out again.

Sometimes – when you can hear happy laughter in the distance – you may feel a bit lonely sitting among the old sandwiches, yet you may also enjoy a moment's peace for yourself too. But you are available if they come back and want you to come and see the amazing discovery – then you go with them and allow them to tell you about it. It's their adventure and this will help them develop confidence and self-esteem.

This picture is a metaphor for the whole of childhood; you are still sitting on that picnic rug when they go off to sixth form college. They may stay away longer but don't be surprised if there are wobbles at any point when they need a cuddle and support. And don't forget they will always need to know where you are, even when they are far away.

Moving on

Every time a child moves on a stage in life, whether it is a new school, new club, starting puberty, moving house, taking exams, or changing friendships, they will regress a little and need you to be the emotional rock again. What sometimes hurts the parent is that children then seem to surge forward sharply and drop that loving embrace without warning, which can feel like a rejection. But it isn't. They're just running off from the rug again finding their own way, knowing that you are there.

Sometimes when children of this age start teasing or criticising their parent's humour, dress sense, or dancing, it can feel again 'hurtful'. But it could be read as a compliment. A child who dares to tease their parent is a secure one who knows they will not be rejected and can come back to the picnic blanket any time they want.

Now apply that image to your adolescent. Think of you and your home as the picnic blanket. Your teenager will be exploring new ways of dressing, socialising, thinking and behaving. But don't assume these are a rejection of the intrinsic you – they are explorations and discoveries and if you give your teenager the chance, they will happily share these innovations with you, and when the innovating gets too much, will still feel able to come back and curl up again, remembering the comfort of being a child.

Even so, encouraging this behaviour is not to diminish the need for family and personal boundaries. This isn't a rallying cry for anything goes.

Remember what we said about boundaries being like belts which can extend and stretch to accommodate growth. Your boundaries around staying out late may indeed get stretched to allow 11 p.m. or midnight curfews as your child grows up, but they will still be firm when it comes to keeping in contact, not taking risks, not meeting up with strangers from the Internet and other behaviours which could be dangerous.

Staying in touch

Keep in touch – what do we mean by that? Make sure you have regular contact with your child every day; this is where social media can be useful. Send them a text during the day saying 'Hi and a x'. Or leave them a note if you are out first thing and are not going to see them.

Don't be grumpy if you don't get anything back; this is you as a parent holding up a flag, saying, 'I'm here when you need me and I love you.'

Don't overstep

Earlier in this section, we explained Overstepper parents and how you might feel if you recognised that this applied to your own mother or father or caregiver. But even if your own parents weren't Overseppers, are you in danger of being too involved in your own child's life?

It may be an uncomfortable truth that while parents love to hear about every moment of their child's existence (remember when they came home from school in Year One and for the first time, when quizzed on their day, said nothing – and how upsetting this was?) Children are just not into us. Especially in any areas involving our relationships, sex, weight worries and especially not moaning about the other parent.

We're not suggesting that the cold distant parent (Ghost) who never shares is an ideal, but the hard truth is you may be your child's confidante (if they choose), but they are never yours.

In *Saving Private Ryan*, Captain Miller (played by Tom Hanks) explains to one of his men why he never complains about conditions or the army to them. 'I don't gripe to *you*, Reiben. I'm a captain. There's a chain of command. Gripes go up, not down. Always up. You gripe to me, I gripe to my superior officer, so on, so on and so on.'

Of course, a friendly relationship is important and if they do something that emotionally has an impact on you, you can tell them, as that is about your relationship, which might be 'I actually find it hurtful that you talk to me that way in front of your friends'. You are giving them feedback on the impact and what you feel. This is different from 'How dare you talk to me like that in front of your friends!' or slamming out of the room when friends come around. Or banning friends altogether.

It is staying available to your child when they need you and continually working on the quality of the relationship. That grows with their growth in age. Imagine your family are like trees; you want your children to grow up strong and healthy, not in your shadow.

When to step in

Wanting to trust your child is admirable, but caring for them completely is more important. So sometimes you may have to step in – even if it feels invasive – to help them learn about healthy self-boundaries.

> **Draw the Line:** *you are the guardian of their self-boundaries. It is your job to care for and protect those boundaries until they are mature enough to do so themselves.*

For example, children need to learn independence when it comes to homework. A spoon-fed child who never has to make decisions around schoolwork will not learn the self-boundaries they will need around getting tasks accomplished in later life, whether at work or university. However, a parent can still check in to see if homework has been completed and if a child feels happy with their work and progress (as opposed to overwhelmed or resentful). This isn't pushing through their boundary but acting as a guardian to them.

This is even more important when challenging issues arise – for example, sexting. Maybe you think, 'I trust my child not to get involved.' But can you be confident their self-boundary is developed enough for them to stay safe? As a parent, you need to be in discussion with a child and to follow your instincts. Keep communication open and don't be afraid to take action if needed.

Talk to them about real relationships, which means two people actually meeting, not images flickering on a screen.

It's worth pointing out too that while they may believe they can trust the other person, can they really do so and where might the images end up? This is also where a good Wi-Fi boundary in the home can support healthy behaviour. Don't be afraid to turn it off at home at night.

Recognising their qualities

If you are a parent of a teenager, think about the last time you commented on something positive to that child. What did it sound like? Was it unconditional, like: 'I think you are great.' Or even conditional – 'You played well in that match'? We all need recognition as humans and if your child is not getting enough positive recognition from you, they will seek it elsewhere.

Make a plan to start recognising your teen daily in a positive way, even if at times that seems hard, and watch their behaviour improve. Make a note in your Learning Journal of what you could say.

University

When a child leaves for university or that first job many parents feel, think, hope and fear their work is done. Let's look at why this might be true for you in one of these ways.

Start by reflecting on your own experience of leaving home as that will have an effect on how you handle this separation. Were you ready to leave or did you feel nudged out? Do you believe you need to nudge out in turn?

If you could have had a choice about events when you left home, what is the one thing you would do differently? This could be anything from wishing you had picked a university near to home and stayed at home, through to studying or working abroad but didn't because of worry of the impact on those left at home.

With this in mind, when you look at your soon-to-be-independent young adult, how confident are you that your plans for their departure are what they want too? What is the all-round healthiest next step for your child? Are you pushing them to a university at the other end of the country because you had to stand on your own two feet (even if your heart tells you something different)?

Are you pushing them away because that's what everyone else is doing around you (even though your fingers are tightly crossed, hoping they won't go)?

At the other end of the scale, are you encouraging/insisting they stay close to home, when they're itching and ready to go? Are you allowing your judgement to be clouded by fear – perhaps you are convinced they aren't able to cope alone yet, or maybe your fear is of being left behind in turn?

EXERCISE: The 5/5 Plan

Sit down with your young adult and each take a piece of paper and a pen.

Now write down, without discussion, five things you would each like to happen for yourself in the next five years. Think big, think small, think all.

Now grant each other one magic wish to apply to one item on your list to make it happen.

Take it in turns to talk through each item on your lists.

You may be surprised at what is important to your young adult which they may not have articulated before. But this is a good chance to check whether they are going down a path which has been preordained by you, them, school and expectations from any direction (however benign the intention). Don't be afraid to make changes to your plans – changes are the magic wand.

Blended Families

Almost all families have a blended element these days – either a step-sibling, half-brother, adopted, or fostered member. This section inevitably cannot look in depth at all those relationships, many of which are complicated and could benefit from psychotherapeutic intervention. However, it's worth pointing out a few starting places for thought and a few ideas about setting successful boundaries in these relationships.

Historically, the step-parent has been demonised (particularly the mother) through literature and film, which is why we want this to be a section which will help you and not judge you.

First, we want to acknowledge the difficulty of this role – one which you may have welcomed with open arms or as someone who has found themselves in the role through love of the parent. Whatever age you come into that child's (or those children's) life/lives will have a profound effect not only on your life but theirs as well.

We talked earlier about parents holding the united boundary and nowhere is this more important than now. Where this needs to start is not with the child but with the parent. We are not suggesting that the other parent has to 'love' you more than the children, or show you more attention or loyalty. However, as a pair you decide how the family works. You might like to start thinking about this as 'house rules'.

The trickiest conversation is with the parent of the child rather than the children. Step parents can feel guilt and concern at the breakdown of a relationship where children are involved – regardless of blame. They may struggle with moving from one way of being to another, because the new house rules must reflect both of you. This could be particularly hard if you as the step-parent are moving into what was the old family home, and especially if you are bringing a child too.

Draw the Line: *the family relationship from now on is a joint responsibility; you get an equal share in how to make it work.*

EXERCISE: Musical Chairs

Take an uninterrupted hour.

Take two chairs and each sit in the chair (one for the parent, one for the step-parent). The chairs should be placed at a natural, comfortable angle to each other, not facing off across a table like an interview situation, where one might feel under interrogation.

For 10 minutes, talk about what you are going to be doing. Without going into deep detail, talk about how long you have been together, how long you have been living together. What are some of the issues you would both like to resolve? Pick some topics such as bedtimes, manners, acknowledgement of hellos and goodbyes, holidays and write them down.

Now pick one topic to discuss. Let's use 'holidays' as an example.

Perhaps one of you has always gone camping with your children and you love trekking as a family, but the step-parent has never done this and loathes the idea of it. The birth parent may want their children to have the same holiday for the purposes of continuity. The other may want a change and asks why 'should' they go camping?

You are now both going to enter Hollywood. Set a timer for 15 minutes. For that time you are going to role play each other.

Stand up and swap chairs. Address each other by your own name.

Talk about the holiday issue as each other, what it means to you and how you feel about it. You both have a responsibility to stay on task (even if you giggle, stay in role). Even if the other says something as the other you don't agree with, stay in role.

After 15 minutes – be boundaried with your time – swap back. Now have a few minutes of silence. Consider what you've heard, how you feel and use this as a basis for your discussion. Do you have a sense of how the other feels?

How might this way of talking to each other be broadened out beyond conversations around holidays?

BRING IN THE BOUNDARIES:

Your Blended Family Plan

Call a meeting of all the family members who now share a home to the kitchen table – mid-morning is ideal.

The birth parent could open the conversation by acknowledging that the family unit is looking different. Rather than bumping along with how it is, that parent could say: 'Let's have a fresh restart.'

This is the time to bring up the house rules, making sure the adults maintain that united boundary and support each other (no mention of his/her rules) and invite the children's input and what they may like to add (in an ideal world).

Ask the group if they feel able to stick to these rules. Ask what might get in the way. Everyone has a responsibility to help things harmonise.

Dealing with a step

Now let's assume you have built that united boundary and it is going reasonably well. Here are some tips for relating to the child/children in the equation to help them work with the new boundary.

Don't detach. It may feel easier and safer to be emotionally aloof but this relationship will need work and you can't abrogate that duty without threatening the stability of the whole family. Accept that there will always be a level of resentment or frustration from a child who would prefer their parents to be together (even if it wasn't fun at the time).

Don't be the victim. Sometimes children play up with a step-parent and it can be hard to see they could well have behaved the same way with a birth parent. A tantrum can just be a tantrum, so don't overreact.

Love's burden

Many birth parents find themselves torn between their new partner and their children, unable to satisfy either. You may feel burdened but you are burdened by love. Hold the set boundary in order to maintain the balance. And admit to yourself it's hard and not easy.

Siblings

'Having lots of siblings is like having built-in best friends.'

KIM KARDASHIAN

That sounds perfect, but the reality for many families with siblings is that best friends can very quickly turn into enemies. Sibling rivalry is a real problem in lots of families. In this section we are going to show you how to build better relationships between siblings.

So, what causes sibling rivalry and how can parents use boundaries to try to limit it?

Perhaps the first piece of advice is not to worry too much. There will always be natural competition for believed or perceived scarce resources, in this case your attention. Bear in mind also that once grown up, this relationship will be for them to manage – not your problem. But you can influence their behaviour by using your boundaries earlier on. So that might mean making it clear that when you are focused on one – for perhaps music practice or to plan a birthday party – that other siblings must stand back (and be quiet).

It's OK to have your focus on one at a time. Trying to shine your spotlight on everyone at all times will not only be exhausting for you, but also means that each child never has the full warmth of your attention. The other parent should be sensitive to this and not try to steal some of that attention for themselves, intensifying the rivalry.

If you are a single parent, the challenges are harder. Make sure you are not exhausting yourself. Ask a friend to monitor or babysit one child so you can take another out for proper undivided attention. Be tough with yourself – don't get distracted.

What you want to foster is their healthy relationship, so no playing your children off against each other. And no playing favourites or carving up turf so children are given preordained roles: 'you are the bright child', 'you are the sporty child', 'you are the naughty child'. Treat them equally and let them find their own specialisms. That way they won't have cause to be jealous of each other.

Don't gossip about one to the other, especially as they get older. They won't thank you for creating division.

Siblings in a Ghost family

The 'cavalry' in families like this might be a sibling (not necessarily elder) who steps into the breach, consciously or unconsciously, in an attempt to fill the emotional hole.

While it may be comforting for other children, and supply some comfort to the sibling who steps in too, it can lead to this child being forced into being a mini-parent when they are not ready. If this feels like you, maybe you missed out on a carefree childhood and perhaps believe that vulnerability is something you are not allowed? Once a child learns to be independent it is hard to come back from that place and be close to others.

Generation Stretch

This is the generation most under pressure; you'll know straight away if this is you.

Male or female, it doesn't matter, but you may be caught between parenting young children and caring for elders, or even a four-generational pull: your own father may be in a care home, but your daughter may be giving birth to your first grandchild halfway round the world. Somewhere in this you will possibly still be working and there will be a house to run, friends who may like your support, commitments to charities or clubs or school committees or pets. You may have your own health issues.

In the modern world, Generation Stretch is never allowed to use the Off button. While that is difficult enough when it's connected to work, say, add in the emotional overload of a needy nonagenarian, or a demanding toddler and there's no slack in the system.

So how can a boundary help here? Most of us would say it is impossible not to say yes to these types of demands. When and how can we say no? But think back to the oxygen mask in Step One. It is important to fix on your own before helping others. In other words, retain the self-care self-boundaries.

CASE HISTORY

Susannah came into therapy through a sense and fear of being overloaded. She recounted the last month and how she had found herself being ill, again. Jennie asked her to think back to the first sign of the flu-like symptoms.

Susannah recalled a day when she had felt exhausted and worried that she was about to be ill and decided to attempt to get everything done in order to be ill in peace. This being the week's chores, dry cleaning runs, shopping, and a trip to the local timber merchants for wood for the log fire. Plus her mother had rung, worrying about a prescription and mentioned she needed shopping too. The children also had library books that needed swapping and a friend had asked her to pick up some recipe books.

From a distance it may look clear what Susannah needed to do but when we are caught up it's harder to press the pause button and take stock than it is to just keep going. It's particularly difficult to abandon a schedule if you have set it. Instead the temptation is to schedule in your own illness as though you can control that as easily as a supermarket run.

Susannah sees her mother as her responsibility and is unable to relinquish or discuss this with her partner, so he isn't aware that she is feeling so stretched and has gone to play golf.

The end result of Susannah's inability to say, 'Enough,' and to ask for help is that she became properly unwell with pneumonia and was forced to spend two weeks in bed, at the insistence of her doctor.

When Susannah finally 'gave in' to being ill, she was surprised to see that life carried on: her mother organised shopping trips with friends; her partner sorted out washing, cooking and homework; friends offered to do the school run. Nothing broke.

What Susannah lost was the slightly pleasing feeling of martyrdom which could have told her she was on the Drama Triangle, ignited by that desire to be a Rescuer. What she gained was peace of mind and a chance to model sensible behaviour to her children.

To ensure that she leaves the Drama Triangle for good and moves to the Winner's Triangle she needs to hold on to this experience and not parcel it up with a label on it saying 'extraordinary circumstances' and chuck it in the cupboard of life.

Conclusion

Well done! You have survived the Step about building boundaries with family – something which many of us find hardest to do, as history and societal pressures affect our responses to these relationships. Ingrained loyalty to the tribe can be incredibly hard to overcome, but the reward is the creation of a balanced, supportive environment for you and your most loved ones and we believe will bring you real joy.

Step Four Summary:

- Our need for a fantasy family weakens our ability to create a real one.
- Ditch your preconceptions about what parenting should be like. Enjoy what it is and what it could be. Be happy to be a 'Good Enough' parent yourself.
- Pedestal parents: it's not about demolishing them, but building up your own self-confidence.
- There is no rule that says we must have a relationship with any particular person in our family – regardless of their biological or societal place in our lives.
- To be a good-enough parent means support and encouragement, holding a child's hand when they need it, letting them have a go on their own when they are ready.
- As children get older you can appeal to their heads as well as their hearts.
- If children learn that the boundaries you set for them on sleeping and eating, say, can be easily breached by outsiders, how safe will they be when the bigger issues come along?

- Don't assume your child always enjoys a lack of boundaries.
- You are the guardian of a child's self-boundaries; it is your job to care for and protect those boundaries until they are mature enough to do it themselves.
- In blended families, children's boundaries are a joint responsibility.

Conclusion

When we started writing this book, neither of us realised how much the process would affect us in practical terms: almost the very first boundary we had to consider was the one around starting a project of this size. We had to carve out a weekday (Mondays) and commit to that being a writing day. This meant turning down other work at times, but it helped us to stay focused.

We were also firm with our boundaries during that day: we took a 30-minute walk before lunch and used that as a time to talk about life rather than the book, and we ate a healthy meal of soup and salad sitting at a kitchen table, not munching at our desks as we worked.

One unexpected consequence of being so boundaried with the process was that for Victoria, the year of writing a self-help book quickly morphed into a year of personal growth too.

When we wrote about self-boundaries early in the book, she found herself challenging her own habits. A good example is sleep. Always an insomniac, she started applying Jennie's sleep tips and bringing in the boundaries around bedtime which proved effective. She now finds she can soothe herself back to sleep on even the most restless night.

Sometimes Victoria admits she has felt as though in a crash

course of life appraisal. For the first time, in many cases, she felt she understood other people's behaviour and where her own responses came from – good and bad.

We both feel it has been a very special experience to find ourselves writing a book together and we are excited to see how *Boundaries* will help others.

So, as suggested at the start, if you follow the Steps in the book and really engage with the exercises and Learning Journal you will feel more comfortable in your own skin and at peace with yourself before long. We are confident, too, you will be more empowered and able to say 'No' to those competing demands which feel so impossible to us all at times. Best of all, you will have gained control over your life and your time – and feel the benefits and true bliss of boundaries.

APPENDIX 1

Transactional Analysis: An Overview

Throughout this book we have been drawing on the theory of Transactional Analysis (TA). So here we give a brief overview.

Transactional Analysis was developed by psychiatrist Eric Berne in the Sixties and is one of the most accessible forms of modern psychology; TA explores and attempts to quantify what underpins human relationships.

Berne devised the idea that a transaction is a unit of social intercourse. So when two or more people encounter each other, sooner or later one of them will speak or give some indication of acknowledging the presence of the other. This is called a *transactional stimulus*.

The other person will then say or do something which is in some way related to the first stimulus and that is called the *transactional response*. (Think of those standard British greeting/response lines: 'How are you?' and 'I'm Fine'.) In order to understand ourselves and our relationships it can really help to understand why we think and behave as we do; what's driving our responses.

In TA we start with the idea of 'self' and, depending on what we are doing and who we are with, this 'self' is not just one fixed way of being. We are made up of different ways of being, thinking and feeling. These are called 'Ego States'. Everybody moves between different Ego States – whether awake or asleep. Clearly, the more we can understand them, the more we understand ourselves.

When we introduced the idea of your debating table (see page 21) we were introducing you to TA and Ego States, so here is the theory behind this concept.

Parent Ego State (P)

When we are in our Parent Ego State we may behave in a Parental manner – drawn to nurture others (as a Parent might) or we may want to tell them off. This is the behavioural side of the model. Both have a positive and negative side. For example, the nurturing side can become overly nurturing of others – even if it isn't wanted and it is at a cost to the giver. Remember the Rescuer? Equally, the controlling side might be viewed as negative, but again the reverse can be true – as children we needed the firmer boundaries at times. Think of a child refusing to go to school: as a parent you know they are not poorly and if you acquiesce it will make the next day even harder for them. To be firm but kind will be more beneficial to the child than overly nurturing and giving them a day off.

But we have a deeper structural side to Ego States. This is where we have been influenced by those who raised us: parents, grandparents, foster parents – indeed any older people of influence.

TA is not an excuse to lay your problems or frustrations at your parents' door though. It's simply acknowledging that our parents have a role to play in creating our beliefs, and that we have a role in choosing which messages we take on. So this is not about looking for excuses, it is about taking responsibility for yourself.

Turning into our parents

In our Parent Ego State we may share or reject cultural views, political views, religion, work ethic, ideas on how to parent and how to fit into society. And there are times, especially as you get older, that you have a thought or say something which reminds you of your parents and their views, even if it is unwelcome. Yet, out it pops.

We mentioned messages we have chosen; this is an important point. Each child in a family will take on different messages – that is because we are all individuals. Each of us growing up decides how to be, in order to fit in with our surroundings.

Here in the Parent Ego State we learn how well to look after ourselves and others. It is also where we can be critical and controlling of others – it's a broad brush but if you hear yourself saying 'You should have tried harder' to yourself or another, this is your Parent Ego State talking. A 'should' or 'ought' is a Parental order.

Child Ego State (C)

The Child Ego State contains the thinking, feelings and behaviour of our childhood. It can be rebellious – wanting to stomp out of a room or slamming the door. Or we may be drawn to be pleasing and to try to make others happy. This is called an 'Adaptive Child' response (we are *adapting* to the other). Or we may be walking down the beach on a sunny day and feel so full of *joie de vivre* that we dive into the sea – this is the action of our 'Free Child'.

There is also a deeper structure to our behaviour in the Child Ego State. This is created by our actual childhood. So a smell or a tone in another's voice can ping us back to feeling 6 years old again. People sometimes say they have a lot of blanks in their childhood.

Don't worry about this. Trust what you remember and trust what you feel when you get triggered into a past memory.

Our Child Ego State is a product of our past and how we chose to be; as well as how we were influenced by others, even how child-like we were allowed to be.

Sometimes circumstances take over. A child has to deal with grown-up problems suddenly – death or serious illness in a parent. How often have you heard it said: 'When that happened, I grew up overnight'?

For someone with that experience they may not know their Child Ego State very well, yet somewhere there may still be a yearning to be carefree, to be looked after and to have fun.

You may be feeling happier or more positive when we talk about the Child. Or perhaps you found more instinctive connection when we were discussing the Parent: 'That sounds like me'. Perhaps you were already setting one against the other – 'Oh, how could anyone behave like that' or 'I could never behave like that'. But be aware whatever you feel now – or where you instinctively identify or recognise yourself most – neither Parent nor Child state is preferable; they all serve a purpose and we need to draw on them all at different times.

Adult Ego State (A)

The fundamental difference between this and the Parent and Child Ego States is that these are both archaic positions. The Adult is here and now. This is the state we wish to get to. But before we can function fully from this state, we need to understand our past and the contents of our other Ego States.

This is why we placed the Adult Ego at the head of the debating table; we need to understand our many selves and learn to listen to them. It is from this place that we can take the healthiest, wisest decisions.

A Question of Transactions

Remember what we said about transactions – those moments between humans when we interact with each other – be it conversation, face-to-face, e-mail, phone or text?

If you are in your Parent state when that transaction occurs, you are inviting either a Parental or a Child response from the other.

If you are in a Child Ego State, you are expecting a Child or Parental Ego State reply from the other. Yet if you are in your Adult Ego State, it invites the other into Adult and keeps both in the here and now. That transaction (or conversation) handled with empathy can then be the most honest way forward as neither party is slipping into their archaic selves.

However, there are occasions when you may be in your Adult Ego State, but the people you are transacting with will stay resolutely in Parent or Child. This is called a crossed transaction and leads to a breakdown in communication or the other party shifting Ego to complement the transactions and keep the contact.

This doesn't necessarily mean the healthiest response though. Maybe you are talking to your boss about holiday leave and you start in Adult knowing that you are entitled to leave, but your boss could respond with a Parental tone of 'You know we are stretched at the moment – do you really have to take leave now?'

They have crossed the transaction and you may feel pulled to be 'good' and respond with a child-like pleasing response of, 'OK,

I'll leave it for now.' This may make the transactions feel easier but where is your healthy self-boundary? Who is caring for you?

By staying in Adult and responding that you are aware it is a difficult time but you will be putting in for your leave nonetheless, which will in the long run be better for all – yes, even the boss – you will not end up an overtired and resentful employee or start looking for another job.

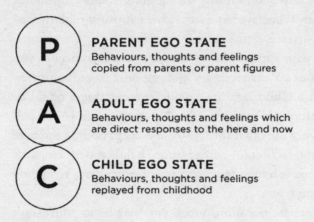

P PARENT EGO STATE
Behaviours, thoughts and feelings copied from parents or parent figures

A ADULT EGO STATE
Behaviours, thoughts and feelings which are direct responses to the here and now

C CHILD EGO STATE
Behaviours, thoughts and feelings replayed from childhood

E is for empathy

How often have you heard or uttered the phrase: 'I know just how you feel'? But how rarely is that true. We all think we know what empathy is and how to use it, but do we?

Often we mistake feeling sorry for another's misfortune as empathy – but that is *sympathy*. Instead, empathy is an awareness of what the other person is feeling even when you cannot relate to that feeling directly – and being aware that our actions/speech have an effect on the other.

For example, when we see footage on television of a young

woman who is a refugee, sympathetic you say 'Poor her', which is a very Parental reaction. You may have a more judgemental response: 'Not another one'. This is also sparked from your Parental Ego State. You might even think 'That looks tough but my life is worse' – a classic Child response.

Empathetic you – in your Adult Ego State – says: 'What an awful thing to experience. I wonder how she is coping? How would I cope? What can I do?' So empathy isn't about saying 'Poor you' or 'Poor me (I have it worse)', but 'I care about you and I care about me'.

Empathy used in boundary-making says: 'I'm aware of my boundary and how it may have an effect on you'. It has great power.

APPENDIX 2:

Strokes

'You can stroke people with words'

F. SCOTT FITZGERALD

You may have heard the word 'stroke' used in the context of a reward; you may even have used it colloquially, too – 'I'm getting my strokes from this'. But what does it mean in TA theory and how does it fit into a book on boundaries?

The classic definition of a stroke is 'a unit of recognition' (Berne, 1972), be it positive or negative. This stems from the importance of a baby to be in contact with their primary caregiver. Babies may be fed and watered and warm and dry, but if they don't have visual and physical contact it's been shown that their health will deteriorate as scientists who studied the Romanian orphans of the 1980s discovered. Hence the word 'stroke' – think cuddling or physically comforting an infant.

Imagine a child on a fairly typical trajectory through their life. They receive cuddles and visual contact from their caregiver, which progresses to the first stages of oral communication (their 'coo's and 'da's get responded to). In this happening, the child knows they exist. As they progress they begin to hear the words 'I love you', which are the ultimate unconditional stroke. Strokes come in different packages from the unconditional through to the conditional – such as being told, 'He's such a good little boy when he eats his food.'

As strokes are such an important part of our wellbeing, if a child is in a place with access to few positive strokes, they will invite negative strokes through bad behaviour because in that moment when the parent turns and shouts at them, it is more than their parent's attention they seek, it is confirmation of their own existence.

Parents ideally want to provide our children with *unconditional* positive strokes but as we live in the real world we all know this isn't always possible. Where it begins to have a potentially negative impact on a child is a repeated conditional stroke such as giving the child attention and praise for good results at school as they will hold on to that (potentially taking it into adulthood, only accepting strokes which are conditional to their good work). As the child grows it is important to maintain the unconditional strokes and the cuddles. And to not be gender specific – i.e. boys get strokes for being brave and not crying and girls get their strokes for being pretty. Different cultures will also have the different learned cultural strokes.

Physical and emotional stroking provides stimuli that are needed in infants to aid growth in the central nervous system. Seeing mammals in the zoo – like chimps and gorillas – reinforces this for us. Watch how tenderly the mother literally strokes and touches her young.

The most recent work on the Romanian children, published in 2015 and reported in the *Daily Telegraph*, is a 12-year study by Harvard University and Boston Children's Hospital in the US, which found that the brains of the orphans stopped developing properly after they were abandoned in the Bucharest institutions. Their 'white matter' – the part of the brain which helps neurons communicate – was significantly damaged by their ordeal, leading to poor language skills and decreased mental ability.

So ideally a child will grow to a backdrop of varied and positive strokes, and not only positive ones but genuine ones. As adults, we can sometimes spot a false stroke – in TA these are called 'Plastic strokes' – a positive gesture which is clearly insincere, like flattery.

Reverse strokes

If you are a parent, you probably know the moment a child says they love you – and means it. It feels good. It could also be called a reverse stroke because these strokes are as powerful for the giver as the recipient. They are a unit of a positive interaction.

And this is an important part of any relationship – not only to give strokes but also to receive them. You may compliment a friend on how well they are looking. If the friend responds jokingly with, 'Oh, you must need your eyesight tested,' you may both laugh but actually your stroke is being rejected.

And if you clock how that feels there will be a distancing between the two of you. Whereas if the friend responds with a heartfelt 'thank you' it brings the two of you closer.

Marshmallow strokes

These sound like a positive stroke but are again insincere. Think of a smile that doesn't quite reach the eyes, or a stiff cold hug.

We may go fishing sometimes for a stroke, by offering one out first – saying 'you look great' and expecting the reply, 'so do you'. But notice how this feels. The lack of genuine motive reduces the value of these strokes.

Stroke filter

Anyone who missed out on those early strokes may be going through life with a 'stroke filter' switched on, unable to accept a genuine compliment or hear themselves praised, accept a hug, or even ultimately be loved. But their filter may be set to accept negative strokes.

What is a self-stroke?

How often do you acknowledge to yourself that you have done a good job – be that at work or as a professional parent or something else? Do you spend more time liberally applying yourself with negative strokes? Is there any room for some positive ones?

If you learnt throughout this book that you have a strong internal controlling parent, you may realise that giving yourself a nice positive stroke is something that hardly, if ever, happens.

On the other hand, you can take steps to change this by learning to give yourself the sort of positive self-strokes you might have received from your parent had they been more nurturing.

Deciding to stop work and go for a run or to go and have that hot bath is a positive self-stroke. There is also the ultimate unconditional positive stroke of being able to acknowledge you like or even love yourself.

The Stroke Clue

Like Christmas presents, we nearly all give others the strokes we would like to receive. So if we miss intellectual praise, we may lavish that on others as it feels good to recognise this kind of prowess in others, even if we are not hearing it at home. This is different from fishing for compliments, because we probably don't acknowledge that that is what we are doing.

Why not take this moment to ask your loved ones what strokes they would like from you and tell them what strokes you would like in return?

It isn't easy to predict what strokes individuals need. Take the glossy, groomed wife who seems to beg attention for her good looks and high-maintenance approach. Often this type of woman really wants strokes from her partner that are connected to her intelligence, skills as a mother, or wit.

EXERCISE: The Stroke Audit

Now take a few minutes to think back to your childhood.

- Do you remember the cuddles – did there come a point where they stopped? Do you remember the unconditional stroke of 'I love you'? Did you get achievement strokes?
- Did you get strokes for swallowing your feelings?
- From that, what strokes do you like now? What strokes do you let in? And what strokes do you give out?
- What is the highest compliment you could pay or receive?

You can never spoil a child with too much love or too many genuine strokes. Because a child who grows up with enough healthy meaningful strokes from infancy will not be fearful of a clear, boundaried relationship with a parent. There will be no instinctive need on their part to push boundaries simply to get their needs met.

Extrapolate this out to your other relationships; where you offer and receive genuine and fair strokes from family, friends and even work colleagues, you will find boundaries are more natural and easier to establish and keep.

Acknowledgements

We'd like to thank profoundly everyone who has supported us in the process of writing this book, particularly:

Gordon Wise, our sagacious agent, who patiently guided us through the whole experience, making it remarkably enjoyable, straightforward and tension-free.

Lisa Milton and Rachel Kenny who understood the concept of boundaries from day one and have never wavered in their enthusiasm for the book.

Kate Latham for her meticulous copy editing, indeed everyone in the HQ family who have taken such great care of us and of our work.

C and N – our greatest advocates, wisest counsel and most fearless supporters.

And lastly C, C and R. We hope you have been inspired to follow your own dreams – however great – by watching these many

many words, phrases and sentences bud, blossom and grow into the chapters of a book.

> 'The most difficult thing is the decision to act, the rest is merely tenacity. The fears are paper tigers. You can do anything you decide to do. You can act to change and control your life; and the procedure, the process is its own reward.'
>
> AMELIA EARHART

LEARNING JOURNAL

INDEX